Decoding Your Destiny

Keys to Humanity's Spiritual Transformation

Tanis Helliwell

Book design by Janet Rouss, cover illustration by Anne Heng

Library and Archives Canada Cataloguing in Publication

Helliwell, Tanis
    Decoding your destiny : keys to humanity's spiritual transformation / Tanis Helliwell. -- Rev. ed.

Includes bibliographical references.
ISBN 978-0-9809033-6-2

1. Spiritual life. 2. New Age movement. I. Title.

BF1999.H44 2011   299'.93   C2011-904267-3

Published by Wayshower Enterprises
www.iitransform.com

Printed and bound in the United States

Decoding Your Destiny

Keys to Humanity's Spiritual Transformation

Tanis Helliwell

Wayshower Enterprises

Table of Contents

LIST OF EXERCISES

Acknowledgments

I wish to thank all beings who are wayshowers on the path to consciousness.

Monika Bernegg made wonderful editorial suggestions in both English and German materials. My gratitude to Carol Sill who practiced true co-creation in the editing of the manuscript and for her encouragement in asking me to share my personal stories. Thanks also go to Janet Rouss for her superb design which caused me to journey higher into truth. I am grateful to the focalizers in our International Institute for Transformation for encouraging me to teach this information, and to Ann Mortifee, Simon Goede, Bob Silverstein and Ruth Dees for helping me to anchor this information in terms most spiritual questers understand.

Poems that introduce all sections are from my book *Embraced by Love*.

Author's Note to the Reader

Currently, the Earth is experiencing a quantum jump in its evolution, a raising of its frequency. We humans, who are cells in the body of the Earth, must also attune to this frequency in order to live on this planet. There is mounting scientific, prophetic, intuitive evidence, as well as just good old common sense, to support this claim. We have three choices: ignore the evidence in hopes we can continue our life as before, panic and vacillate about what to do to survive physically, or transform ourselves physically, emotionally, mentally and spiritually in order to align with this new frequency.

This process is in keeping with the natural and spiritual laws on which our world is founded. Great wayshowers, such as Krishna, Isis, Buddha and Christ show us the way. Likewise, information is available from religious traditions, myths, science, dreams, and our own intuition to show us the way to transform ourselves. *Decoding Your Destiny* can assist individuals with this transformation, which is as beautiful and profound as when a caterpillar transforms into a butterfly.

The greatest factor that limits us is the collective hypnosis in our everyday life about what is real. In this third dimensional reality we too easily rely on our physical senses of sight, hearing, touch, and taste to determine reality even though our greatest mystics have consistently said that this world, as perceived by these senses, is an illusion. Science has finally agreed with these mystics and stated that we are 99.9 percent ether, or space, yet most of us are still unable to see or recognize Sally, Joe and the dog without a solid form.

So we have a dilemma. If we cling to the third dimensional illusion we will find ourselves in an increasingly perilous physical environment with global warming, increased volcanic activity, economic collapse, more guns and violence, food and water shortage and frightening diseases. People usually don't change until the pain of not changing becomes greater than the pain of changing, and that is the situation in which many people find themselves currently.

The good news is that in the last two or three decades there has been an immense increase in interest and information from scientific, psychological, mystical traditions, including TV and films about higher dimensions and different realms of existence. Psychiatrist Carl Jung referred to the next level of consciousness, which humans must access in order to become conscious co-creators, as the collective unconscious. This collective unconscious is the spiritual history of humanity: what we have evolved from, what we are now and what we are evolving into. Biologist Rupert Sheldrake calls this etheric field of energy the morphogenetic field, and the archaeologist, mystic priest Teilhard de Chardin referred to it as the noosphere. Other words for the collective unconscious in the western mystical tradition are the Akashic Records and the Book of Life.

This Book of Life exists in a higher frequency than our third dimensional material world, and, although unseen by our physical eyes, it can be read, heard, and felt with our spiritual senses. For example, we cannot see radio waves and yet we can tune in different radio stations to listen to a variety of programs. So with our spiritual senses: we can attune ourselves to various frequencies to access the information about the spiritual history of our Earth, humanity and even ourselves. These records exist, like dreams and thoughts, on higher frequencies than our physical reality. It is essential to become aware of this, for the lower frequencies, where thoughts of scarcity, greed, lust, self-pity and anger exist, are responsible for the collective hypnosis of our material world.

There is more good news. By raising our frequency we can see our own programming and we can change it not only for ourselves, but also for others. Each person who raises his or her frequency increases exponentially the ability for others to do so as well. Furthermore, when we rise to higher frequencies, we know at a cellular level that our thoughts determine our reality, and that we can create any reality for our world that we can envision. This means that we are able to create a world at peace with all beings living in harmony. The information in this book is derived from these higher frequencies. I published some of this information in a different form in 1988 and have been teaching and working with this material since then to anchor it is this third dimensional reality. I believe that this new more in-depth and accessible version will assist you to increase your frequency through the law of harmonic resonance.

Decoding Your Destiny is a road map for humanity, an encyclopaedia for our spiritual evolution, and what we need to know

NOW to consciously evolve. It looks at the signposts from the Christian, Buddhist, Native American religious traditions, psychology, myths, as well as archaeological, astrological and scientific data in order to demonstrate the similar truths at the heart of all these paths. It discusses the many beings, including the Creator, Angels, and beings of the inner Earth, who have interacted with humanity from our earliest prehistory until today—and even into our future and their relationship with us. This book deals with previous cycles of human evolution, including mythic Lemuria and Atlantis. It examines the cycle we are now entering—that of the enlightened human; and suggests what each of us can do as a conscious co-creator on Earth. The signs are obvious that our old reality is ending and that it is urgent that we embrace the new emerging world order. But how? *Decoding Your Destiny* gives you specially designed exercises to do individually and/or in groups to assist you on this journey.

Tanis Helliwell, Diamond Heart, November 2011

Section One

HUMANITY'S NEXT EVOLUTIONARY STEP

Rebirth

Do not second-guess spirit;
your lists of preferences
mean nothing.
Spirit is not interested in your comfort,
but in breaking you apart
until your shell crumbles
and you are reborn as love.

Five Levels of Consciousness

At this time in humanity's development, many people are experiencing dislocation and confusion about their roles in society, their family and even themselves. It may appear to them that their former roles, values, and relationships are no longer valid. They question the purpose of their lives and everything that once had meaning for them.

What I am discussing is far more than a mid-life crisis, for it may occur at any age from a teenager to octogenarian. This process may commence suddenly with the onset of a life threatening illness or it may be a gradual disenchantment with society's values in someone who "has it all." Individuals may be uninterested in spiritual topics and still encounter this process. Whether consciously aware of it or not, all people are spiritual just as they are physical, emotional, mental. Therefore, this experience may arise both in the life of someone who meditates and does spiritual practices, or with someone who does not. It is not our personality, our lower self, which decides the timing of our awakening but our higher self, our soul.

This process is predictable and inevitable and will ultimately happen to each of us. As individuals undergo this spiritual crisis, it feels as if they are losing control of their lives and losing everything that gave their lives meaning and identity. This feeling, however, is just their personality's fear of losing control. Actually it is an indication of spiritual and personality maturity when an individual experiences this spiritual crisis.

References to this process are found in many religions and cultures. In the Old Testament of the Bible it is referred to as the dark night of the soul. The twenty-third psalm speaks of this journey as going through the valley of the shadow of death. In ancient Greece, Egypt, India and other cultures there were schools of wisdom that helped individuals through this process. These individuals were taken into seclusion and taught what was referred to as the inner mysteries, the spiritual truths on which our world is founded. This was done in order to protect them from others and the outer world, as it is a time when all previous learning falls away and they stand naked, unknowing and vulnerable. During this transition stage individuals are unlearning old patterns of thinking and feeling, and learning new ones. It's possible, therefore, that they may mislead others with partial information and interfere with the life purpose of another person. So, keeping them in seclusion in ancient cultures was a way to protect them from others and others from them. At the end of the transition, these individuals re-enter the everyday world more conscious of their purpose and how to accomplish it in their work in the world.

Individuals might encounter a series of dark nights of the soul over this or several lives in order to arrive at this higher level of consciousness. In our modern western world, there is little support for people to undergo this transformation. Very few enjoy the luxury of quitting their jobs and going to India for the rest of their life to meditate. Nor is this necessary. None of us are given more than we can handle. We are set up to succeed in this transformation and not to fail. This means that if we are married, have children, and have nine–to–five jobs, we can do this and still succeed. This is likewise true even if we are divorced, childless, and have just been fired from our job. Each of us, as painful as it might seem, is given just what is needed to assist us with our transformation. This series of changes is recognized in some traditions as the third initiation. Whatever it may be called, these are steps that we take in order to arrive at a higher level of consciousness.

One of the reasons that so many humans are rising to the third level of consciousness at this time is that the Earth is rising as well. Anything that affects the Earth affects humanity. The Earth is a living being, which is holding itself back from moving to the third level of consciousness until the majority of humans are able to do this as well.

These next two thousand years, which are known as the Aquarian Age, can be said to be the time of the enlightened human, the water bearer who pours the water of life onto the Earth. This is the sign of the conscious human who is dedicated to world service, the human who lives and works in the third level of consciousness. During these next two thousand years, the majority of humans will do this so that the Earth will be able to continue with its evolution. Humans and the Earth become conscious partners in this process during this time.

The Earth is surrounded by a protective energy that has been metaphysically called a "ring-pass-not". This ring is like a shell, which encases the Earth and separates it from all the other conscious planets in our solar system. This shell is now cracking and new energies are entering from more conscious planets in our solar system, from our own sun, and from other solar systems that are more highly evolved than ours. These energies have never existed on our planet before and are greatly accelerating the development of consciousness here.

The ring-pass-not is cracking like the shell around an egg when the chicken is ready to hatch. These cracks put a strain on all of the Earth's systems. Physically, it can mean increased volcanic activity, earthquakes and climate changes. Emotionally, it is demonstrated through violence, depression and mood swings, such as manic depression, among the Earth's inhabitants. Mentally, it is revealed through the collapse of old structures, such as our economic, family and religious systems based on old values and roles. Spiritually this entails a rise in spiritual interest and consciousness amongst humans around the world.

As the Earth moves to a higher frequency, all beings on its surface must do so as well. Each of us, like the Earth, has a shell that surrounds us until we move to the third level of consciousness. This shell is composed of our physical, etheric, emotional and mental bodies that form the personality vessel. When this personality is mature—as with the chick in its shell—the vessel will crack. The cracking is what we associate with the dark night of the soul: when we feel that we are no one, doing nothing, going nowhere. This cracking is necessary so that the soul can merge with the personality. Through this process we become what's called a soul-infused personality, meaning that the soul works through the personality to serve in the world.

On moving to the third level of consciousness our physical, etheric, emotional and mental bodies start blending together. In addition, the boundary between ourselves and others starts to disappear. It is as Jesus said, "What you do to the least of my brothers you do to me." Without the shell surrounding us, we discover that we are part of every other living being on this planet. This experience is so radically different from the dominant one prior to our transformation—in which we are separate and different from others—that our life will never be the same. With this realization we cross the threshold into becoming a conscious co-creator who works with the spiritual laws on which our world is founded.

Decoding Your Destiny gives you seeds of information to start new patterns in thinking so you are able to access this third level of consciousness. It gives you keys to eliminate what is no longer needed in your life and to manifest what is. It is necessary to be in this higher state of consciousness if you want to be a conscious co-creator on this planet and to use the spiritual laws to create physically, emotionally, and mentally what is in accordance with divine will. Humans are creators, whose thoughts determine the third-dimensional world in which we live. However, most of what we create is unconscious. Our buildings, organizations, newspapers, computers are all products we have created. Some of our creations have great value, some have less, and some are counterproductive to life on this planet.

Three Areas of Transformation

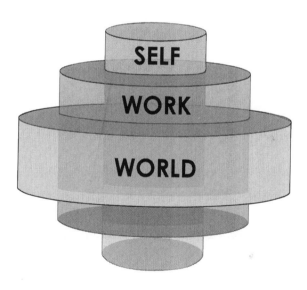

Figure 1 - The interrelationship between self, work and world.

Co-operating with spiritual and natural laws in our everyday world is the key! To become conscious co-creators with these laws, we need to function consciously in three areas of our life, which are self, our work or job, and our commitment to the world. The third level of consciousness entails a commitment to world service even if this is with our own family. To achieve this goal, we must first transform ourselves so our fears, attachments and self-interest do not sabotage the effectiveness of our work in the world. We affect others not only by what we do, but also by who we each are as individuals. The more we purify our own personality vessel, the greater our positive impact on others by our very presence. But where will we find the methods and knowledge to purify ourselves? This knowledge is found in spiritual traditions, in myths, in dreams, in meditation, and in many transpersonal psychological disciplines.

Although the final result in attaining the third level of consciousness is increased love, trust, harmony and compassion for others, there may be pain and difficulties on the journey, as people leave their more material attachments behind. Yet, the numbers of individuals engaged in this process are increasing daily. This is obvious from the chronic low-grade depression we sense in people who have fine homes, jobs, cars and the opportunity to buy most anything they wish. A soul hunger is emerging in people in the western world who have strengthened their personality and fed it everything it wishes. No amount of possessions, relationships, or status will fill this hunger. Because so many people are undergoing this spiritual transformation at this time in history, it is creating a higher frequency in the collective unconscious of humanity. This momentum is increasing both the speed at which people are able to move to the third level of consciousness, and also the numbers of humans achieving it.

It is only when we are able to maintain the third level of consciousness that we are able to fully become world servers because, until then, we haven't yet achieved our own physical, emotional and mental stability. Our commitment to serve others above serving ourselves will be tested throughout the process until our foremost goal is to serve the divine will on Earth. It is still possible to lead an ordinary life with family and career, but our major concern is no longer with money, status, and security, but rather with a desire to assist others. Our joy comes predominantly through learning, loving and sharing. In my work, both as a management consultant and psychotherapist specializing in spiritual transformation, I have found that spiritual transformation does not begin until individuals have learned how to hold down a job and have successful relationships with others. This means they have a degree of personal maturity.

About half the folks embarking on the spiritual path do so because they are unhappy in their work and the other half feel unfulfilled in their personal life. To assist both of these groups I wrote a practical, how-to-book called *Take Your Soul to Work*, which has exercises to help people to discover and then manifest their purpose in life in the material world. Both of these groups also feel a need to help the Earth and for their lives to make a difference. This is a soul call. Ultimately the starting point is unimportant and individuals come to realize that transformation occurs on all three levels: self, work and world.

It is most common for this soul call to come in your forties, however for me, as for many others, my soul call came very early in life. As a mystic I found that none of the common jobs that existed for women in my youth, such as teacher, secretary, nurse or flight attendant, would make use of my special talents. Sure I could do them if I applied myself, however only 25 to 50 percent of who I really was could be used in those jobs. Since my teens I worked in my parent's hardware store, factories, food service industry, mental health hospitals, and eventually became a secondary school teacher and counselor. As such I mastered the real world and by age 25 had paid off my student loans for my Masters degree, owned a house in Toronto, had a common-law partner and good friends. Luckily, I was fired for being too radical and Bill and I decided to take a break from work and travel around the world for a few years.

By the time I returned home in my late twenties I had been meditating for several years and had a strong hunger to connect even more deeply with spiritual realms. At the same time I had good self-esteem from my previous success in the material world. This combination allowed me to risk self-employment where half my time I offered spiritual programs—such as tours to sacred sites and past life regressions—outwardly in the world. The other half I worked as a management consultant with companies like IBM and banks in the area of personal and leadership development. This served to keep me grounded and living in the world as a normal person and allowed me to reach individuals working in large organizations who ordinarily would not be caught dead speaking with a psychic or mystic.

The reason I am mentioning my own life is to help you to realize how my spiritual calling to help the world and all beings has been intricately connected to my chosen work in the world. As I transformed personally in my inner world through meditation, doors closed in the outer world, such as being a secondary school teacher. However, other doors opened. This is normal and, although painful at the time as no one likes rejection and failure, these things are necessary to keep us moving to fulfill our soul's purpose.

So back to you! The exercises that you will find throughout this book will assist you in applying the information we are discussing in your life. Completing these exercises will increase and stabilize your frequency at a higher level of consciousness depending on the degree of inner searching you engage in to complete them. Simple yes and no answers will seldom take you far. I recommend that you work through these questions in a journal and read this book slowly so that you can allow the questions and your answers to work on you for several days before moving on to the next exercise. This means to dive deeply and honestly into your depths and to realize there is not a right or wrong answer, only your answer. Honesty with yourself will help you to peel back your layers to uncover your soul essence and gifts.

Please start by recording the answers for Exercise 1 in your journal. Follow this procedure for each of the exercises included in *Decoding Your Destiny*.

Exercise 1: Transformation in Self, Work and World

Take a moment to still your mind before contemplating your answers to each of these questions and record your observations in your journal.

- ❖ What inner and outer actions are you taking to transform yourself to a higher level of consciousness? Examples could be meditation, self-help books, courses.

- ❖ Describe ways that your work helps others and the world? Examples could be that the services you provide, such as environmental, actually help the world.

- ❖ What other activities do you do to benefit the world? Examples could range from volunteerism, recycling at home or work, or caring for an aging parent.

Some human beings have not consciously started their spiritual journey, but the majority have. Many individuals are still in the first level of consciousness, which is learning the physical laws of survival and of controlling the physical desires of their body. Fewer individuals are in the second level of consciousness, which has to do with the control of their emotions. These individuals are learning to control their negative emotions: anger, lust, envy, pride, sloth and greed, and find ways to turn this energy into positive feelings. In western Christian tradition these faults are known as six of the seven deadly sins. In the eastern Vedic tradition these negative emotions are known as the six doshas of the ego (personality) when it identifies with the material world. As we see in the classic Indian text, the Bhagavad Gita, these faults must be overcome if we are to know our soul.

Five Levels of Human Consciousness

5th – Unity
Being at one with
Spirit and all Beings

4th – Higher Mental
Living at *cause* and not *effect*

3rd – Lower Mental
Controlling thoughts that create emotions

2nd – Emotional
Controlling anger, lust, envy, pride, sloth and
turning this energy into positive feelings

1st – Physical
Mastering physical urges of sex, sleep and eating

Lives on Earth prior to conscious journey
Developing increased consciousness

Figure 2 - Progress from lower to higher consciousness in five steps in human evolution on Earth.

Still fewer individuals are functioning in the third level of consciousness, which involves controlling the thoughts that create their emotions. As we progress through these levels, we learn to work with higher frequencies moving from the realm of feelings with the second level to the realm of thoughts in the third and fourth levels. The fourth level of consciousness entails controlling the higher mental body. To do this, we must be able to live at cause and not effect by creating the thoughts, and therefore, the life we desire. By the time we move to the fifth level, we are capable of travelling in space and time and recreating our physical body wherever, and whenever, we want. At that level we are one with spirit and all beings. There is no separation.

Consciousness continues to evolve to even higher levels and frequencies, however this is not the focus here. This book is concerned mostly with assisting individuals who are in the second level and wish to move into the third and, to some extent, fourth level of consciousness, which is essential in order to live on the Earth during this current transformation. These levels interpenetrate each other and, depending on our thoughts, we might move from the first to the third level in the space of a few minutes, or vice versa.

When we consciously begin our journey from animal-human to fully human consciousness, the time it takes to move to higher levels decreases. The majority of human beings have been on this planet a very long time and might have incarnated countless times before mastering their physical and emotional urges in the first and second levels of consciousness. Yet, to progress from the second to third level might take only a few incarnations. Why is that?

When we begin anything a great deal of effort is involved, and we have to learn the laws that lead to mastery. Then, all of a sudden, we are not pushing the rock uphill anymore. We now know the laws and have the momentum to complete what we started. Once we begin to move to higher levels of consciousness, a momentum is created because our frequency has increased. Events occur at a faster pace as we move to higher dimensions. We are attuning more to the universal spiritual laws and becoming clearer about what those are. We are also receiving more assistance from those who have walked the path before us—because now we can contact them in higher dimensions and they us—so the process quickens.

It is important to note that presently there are many new souls incarnating called by the name of Indigo, or Crystal, children. Their first incarnation is already on the higher frequencies of the third and fourth levels of consciousness, so they do not go through the lengthy process that those who came up through human evolution needed. More will be said on this in *Enlightened Humans: The Seventh Cycle* on page 104.

Major Issues Facing Individuals

Commitment

The major difficulty that people have in attaining the third level of consciousness is commitment. That is, the commitment to serve the divine will above our own personal will. There are great beings who oversee our evolution, who have designed many tests. These are meant to help us, both in strengthening our weak areas, and in breaking through our shell. The purpose of these tests is to make our personality surrender to divine will. This process is exemplified by the New Testament story of Jesus in the garden of Gethsemane where he knew that his future held much pain and prayed, if possible, to avoid it. In this story Jesus was tested to ensure that he would fully commit to the purpose for which he had come to Earth. Through much wrestling with his personality, which would seek to avoid pain at all costs, he ultimately committed to his soul's purpose with the words, "Not my will but Thine be done." This is the struggle that each of us must undertake to surrender our personality's comforts in order to serve the divine will.

Although the specific tests that each of us undergoes in rising to the third level are unique, the end goal is the same. We are given exactly what is needed in order to crack the shell without destroying the baby chick inside. Some of us might experience the dissolution of a marriage, lose money, or be unfairly accused of something we did not do. But whatever the test, it is perfectly adapted to the needs both of our personality and soul. Our choice is to see these difficulties for what they are—opportunities to learn and grow—or to collapse into self-pity, retaliation and self-righteousness. The choice is ours.

Trust and Fear

To succeed in this journey to consciousness we need to have a deep level of trust in the Divine—whether we call it God or the Creator—to look after us. We also must trust ourselves that we are up to the challenge. Lastly, we need to seek role models, wayshowers, who have walked the path before us. These are Christ, Buddha, Isis, Mary Magdalene and many more. When we trust and surrender to the greater good, we open our hearts in a deeper way than was previously possible. The ability to more deeply love and serve others and the world is birthed out of our own pain.

Through this process a profound opening occurs in our hearts. It is an almost magical experience. We find ourselves in a new place, which we might have consciously, or perhaps unconsciously, yearned for. It's a place of peace, compassion, and acceptance of ourselves and for all beings. To arrive in this place requires a deep surrender to trust that we will be safe, knowing that we are loved and cherished. We see that we are the young brothers and sisters of those who have gone before and who are wayshowers ahead of us on the path. We recognize that our Universe is in a continuous stage of growth, a conscious creation; that the Earth is evolving, that the planets are evolving, that the Sun is evolving, and that we are part of this continual process of evolving into consciousness.

What I am describing exists within the space-time continuum of evolution. In higher dimensions enlightened beings and the Creator exist outside of time. In this state all is eternal present 'Isness'. In this state the Creator and I and you are one. As Jesus states, "My Father and I are one." This is the fifth level of consciousness. Highly evolved Masters, wayshowers who have lived among us, unanimously concur that the third-dimensional world in which we live is not real. Our world is a construct, an illusion. Still, within this construct, which we mistakenly refer to as reality, the Universe, the Earth and humans are evolving. Within this constructed world there is knowledge and there are laws to learn, which will develop us spiritually so we will be able to progress in consciousness.

In this third dimensional reality we cannot help but evolve, and the major way that we hinder our evolution is to keep ourselves closed. What closes us? Fear. Fear that we will not have enough; fear that we will not be looked after; fear that we will not be loved; fear that we will not be smart enough. Fear that we will undergo a scarcity of something, and that we will not receive whatever the goodies are that others are getting. Fear combined with lack of trust in the Divine makes it difficult to commit to do the divine will. Fear shuts down the flow of energy from the higher spiritual realms and impedes the entire process of transformation.

Aligning with our Soul, our Higher Self

The majority of time for most of us is spent in our personalities—our lower selves; we don't have a sense of our higher selves. Almost all of our attention is concerned with the things of the mundane world, such as shopping, doing our laundry, and not having too many onions in our salad. And that is on a good day.

Some days, maybe only one percent of our attention is actually geared to our higher self—our soul. When this occurs, the higher self is relegated to a very small percentage of our time. So, in order to get our attention, it gives us discomfort, because otherwise it is ignored.

The lower self—our personality—seeks comfort and pleasure. "I think I'll have dessert." "I want to go to the movies." "I'll buy this nice dress." "I want to have sex." These are the concerns of the lower self. When we give in to these urges of the personality, our higher self doesn't get our attention at all. So, by making our lives uncomfortable, it gets our attention and we begin to move towards consciousness.

Here are some of the ways our soul, our higher self, makes us feel uncomfortable in order to get our attention:

- It makes us feel guilty. Period.

- It gives us physical discomfort when our physical body is not in alignment with the soul.

- It gives us emotional discomfort and feelings of anger, hurt, envy, self-pity and depression. These negative emotions remind us that we are not serving the higher good, are off track, and are not doing what we are supposed to be doing.

- It gives us thoughts of inadequacy and we compare ourselves negatively to others.

- It makes us feel selfish that we think only of ourselves, and not of the physical, emotional, mental or spiritual welfare of others.

- It makes us feel guilty that we are not meditating or devoting time to our soul's purpose.

It's only when we have discomfort that we start asking, "Where would I find relief from this?" It's like having an itch and wanting to scratch. Sometimes, individuals scratch at their problem until they have an open wound. By doing this, they enlarge the area of pain and discomfort rather than finding and applying the remedy for it. By talking about their pain continually, they activate the thoughtform that has to do with this particular form of discomfort. That's how a thoughtform grows. The solution is to exercise self-discipline in order to hear clearly what the higher self has to say.

Here's a stretching thought. View your discomfort as a sign of progress! Unconscious individuals go along day-to-day without feeling these things. They can be selfish and not feel any guilt. They eat, drink a lot, and might feel bad the next day but they say, "That's fine. I had such a great time" rather than, "Why did I do that to myself?" This self-questioning is a signal that over-indulgence wasn't a good idea. Therefore, when we start feeling physical, emotional, mental or spiritual angst, it is actually positive because it means that our higher selves, our souls, are getting through to us.

When the pain becomes strong enough, we start acting on it. We begin to discipline ourselves to do things that will delay the discomfort. For example, this might be meditating, being kind to others, eating properly and exercising. Partnering our higher selves, our souls, doesn't happen overnight, but the important thing is to become aware of how our souls affect our lives today. There are certain predictable topics that are of interest to individuals rising to the third level of consciousness as they grapple with meaning in life. Even if they were not previously interested in spiritual things, during this process these topics will begin to interest them. By addressing these topics, whether in discussion or in reading, the frequency in these individuals increases so that they open to higher levels of connection to their soul.

Co-creation with Others and The Divine

Thus far, we have been defining the third level of consciousness so that individuals will recognize the signs in both themselves and in others. We have discussed the fact that the Earth is undergoing a similar process, which has led to an increase in the numbers of people rising to the third level. Before the year 2000 most individuals took this journey of transformation alone. Although this route is still available, another route is coming into form, that of conscious co-creating with others.

This entails joining with other like-minded individuals—a soul group of peers—with the express purpose of aiding them, and of them aiding you to attain consciousness. Even though these individuals might be friends or family, it is unimportant that you like them personally. More often than not, the group members have diverse gifts and strengths, and what they hold in common is a desire for world service and a commitment to help others on their spiritual path.

The benefits in being a member of a co-creative community are enormous, as each member amplifies the effects that the group can have on each other and in the world. This greatly increases the strength of the community in manifesting their goals, and decreases the time that would take each individual. To succeed, all members in the co-creative community need to be focused on common goals and must work together to achieve them. If one or two members do not pull their weight, it negatively affects the energy of the others. Co-creation can be seen as the way manifestation is done in higher spiritual realms by the Masters who guide us. So in learning to do this now, we are practicing the method we will use in the near future. This path is available to many people now because so many are moving to the third level of consciousness.

To work co-creatively with others we need to align our vision, focus, commitment, and energy and also deeply trust each group member. We need to send love and energy to them, to the Earth, and even to strangers in the same way that we send it to ourselves. Naturally, each of us has preferences to overcome and the other group members act as role models in how to overcome these. For example, some of us love God unconditionally, but we are not quite sure about our fellow humans. Others might love their families, but they are not quite sure about men, or women, atheists, or Muslims. Ultimately, we must learn to love all equally, and through our fellow group members we learn to do this.

In our International Institute for Transformation we are learning how to co-create together. Our members from very early on, when first coming to the programs, liked the idea, the theory of co-creation, however not all initially understood what they would have to do to be co-creators. Many fell back on "what was in it for them" when asked to do something which entailed a commitment which would not directly benefit them. However, over time and with practice this has changed as they have continued to face their personality attachments and overcome their fears until they have become true co-creators both with the Divine and with their peers.

Nor was I a perfect example of co-creative practice. Because I see people from the soul level I often have unrealistic expectations that others would put the Earth and service to their soul ahead of their personality needs and I was disappointed that this seldom occurred, at least early on in people's spiritual journey. I needed to modify my unrealistic expectations as well as allowing others to fully share their vision, each one of theirs being as valid as mine. In doing so together we have learned greater trust, respect and love of others and ourselves—just as we are.

Exercise 2: Issues of Commitment, Trust and Fear

Take a moment to still your mind before contemplating your answers to each of these questions and record your observations in your journal.

❖ Which is your greatest issue with others: commitment, lack of trust or fear?

❖ How does this affect your life?

❖ What is your soul asking you to do to overcome this issue?

❖ Are there any kinds of people of whom you are intolerant? If so, what can you do to respect and appreciate them fully?

❖ Envision an individual who exemplifies this kind of person. See yourself move from intolerance to appreciation to love.

Section Two

BEGINNINGS IN EVOLUTION

Birth of the Day

Streaming from black-holed space
sunrise fills my face.
Glorious promise of hope,
unceasing new beginnings.
Chirping, cawing, buzzing start:
God opens the day.

The Creator: A Trinity

The three main questions that humans seeking consciousness have asked for millennia are: Where have we come from? Why are we here? Where are we going? Science, history, psychology and religious traditions, all have striven to answer these questions. This book examines our role on this planet through examining our past, present and future from a spiritual perspective. I could say simply, "We are creator gods in training," but this would mean something different to each person. To understand what being a co-creator is, it is necessary to understand how creation fundamentally works. The best place to begin is with the consciousness that created our universe, all life and each of us.

Exercise 3: Your Image of the Creator

Take a moment to still your mind before contemplating your answers to each of these questions and record your observations in your journal.

❖ What is the first image that comes to mind when you think of what the Creator looks like?

❖ Perhaps some of you have a physical image of the Creator. Is it an old man with a beard? Perhaps it is Jesus on the cross. If you are not from a Christian religious tradition you might think of Krishna, Buddha, Shiva, Tara or Jehovah as a super-human type of being. We could continue this line of questioning for some time, and hardly anyone will think of a female figure. Even fewer people will think of the consciousness in nature.

❖ Perhaps you do not perceive a physical image. Could the qualities of your Creator be more definitely male or female?

❖ What are some of these qualities of your Creator?

Is there a Creator, a higher consciousness who created humans and all other beings on the Earth? If so, what is this Creator like? This is the ultimate question asked in our spiritual search as we attempt to determine how to relate to such a being. Meanwhile, where do we find the answers as we move beyond the collective programming of humanity's myths about the Creator?

Even though we know that the Creator does not look like these images it comforts us to personalize and reduce spirit to human proportions so we can relate at our present state of evolution. Even enlightened Buddhists, Hindus, and Christians often use images of the Divine in their meditation as it inspires them to higher awakenings. These embedded human images of the Divine are not the goal but pointers in the direction to go. Science may easily point a finger at these images and assert that it is impossible that our universe was created by anything looking remotely like a human, and in a literal sense how could we disagree. It is for each of us to discover the qualities of the creator and our own divinity through an inner journey. This image of the Divine evolves as we evolve.

Although the Creator encompasses all aspects we know of as he, she and it, for the purpose of this book I'll most often use the pronoun "he" for ease of reading. Even if we do not maintain a visual image of the Creator, we may feel a connection to an older male voice in our heads telling us what to do. The question becomes, "Is there any truth to the images we hold, and what do humans have in common with the consciousness that created us?"

One of the earliest known mentions of the Divine is found in Sanskrit literature. There we find three names to describe the Divine: *Sat, Chit, Ananada*, which may be translated as being, consciousness, bliss outpouring. The first aspect of divinity *Sat* is unknowable, alive, existence. *Chit* is awake, knowing, intelligence. *Ananada* is unconditional love and bliss pouring endlessly through all realms and dimensions. Likewise, in Christianity the Creator is said to be a trinity—that is, the Father, the Son, and the Holy Spirit. These three qualities of the Divine are will, love-wisdom, and active intelligence.

This three-fold Divinity is not a separate being but is present in all beings, in all worlds, and in all dimensions. However, to better understand the Divine it may be helpful to examine each of the three qualities.

The Divine Father

The One was breathing by its own power in deep space. Only the One was: there was nothing beyond. Darkness was hidden in darkness. The all was fluid and formless. Therein, in the Void, by the fire of fervor arose the One. And in the One arose love.
(Song of Creation, Rig Veda)

The One is present beyond time and space and outside of the impulse of evolution. The ancient Vedas call this aspect Brahman, also *Sat*. It is difficult to speak of this first aspect of consciousness as it is outside of words, thoughts, and feelings, outside of the manifested world. It is absolute spirit. This aspect of divinity is whole unto itself.

St. John's Gospel, the most metaphysical of all four gospels, begins, "In the beginning was the Word, and the Word was with God, and the Word was God." This account is distinctly similar to the *Egyptian Book of the Dead*, one of the oldest written texts in the world, which says, "I am the Eternal, I am Ra...I am that which created the Word...I am the Word..."

Physicists, such as Stephen Hawking, speak of two laws that govern our universe. The first one is called the no boundary condition, which is a force with no beginning that has existed forever. This is equivalent to the father aspect of the Creator. The second law is the law of evolution in time, which commenced approximately 14 billion years ago as the big bang. This is the mother aspect of the Creator, one of whose names is Sophia.

Sophia: The Divine Mother

This infinite force who created form in our manifested universe is often seen as the Divine Mother. This is especially true in eastern religions and mystical traditions and less true in conservative Christianity where the Creator, both unmanifested and manifested, are male.

The feminine presence of the Creator is called by many names. In Hindu scripture she is referred to as the Divine Mother and is that aspect of God that is active in creation, the shakti, or the outpouring of the transcendent Creator. Other names for this aspect of divinity are Aum, the cosmic intelligent frequency, or the Divine Word that creates form. In Christianity she is known as Sophia, the Mother of the World.

It is important to note that she is the mother of all life not only on the Earth, but on all planets and solar systems in this galaxy, in all dimensions and all manifested worlds. Sophia is the mother of all form, not only the physical form of nature that we are able to see, but the elements in other dimensions of form. She is the force behind the evolution of consciousness. She is a great cosmic being and mother even to our own planet Earth. She is the cycle of the seasons, and of birth and death and birth again. We have lost touch with the Divine Mother and in so doing have lost touch with our physical bodies and the physical body of the Earth. Now, as a mother sets her destructive child on the right path Sophia is showing us the ecological problems that we have created through erroneous thinking and actions.

In Judaism the feminine presence of the Creator is called the Shekinah. In Christianity, she is the vessel through which the fire of the Holy Spirit awakens consciousness in the world of form. She is the wisdom behind nature and evolution. She is spirit in matter—the spiritual fire in us—as well as the vessel that holds the spirit.

In Proverbs collated about 700 BCE, Wisdom (another name for Sophia), says:

> The Lord created me at the beginning of his work,
> The first of his acts of old.
> Ages ago was I set up, at the first,
> Before the beginning of the Earth.
> When there were no depths I was brought forth,
> When there were no springs abounding with water.
> Before the mountains had been shaped,
> Before the hills, I was brought forth;
> Before he hath made the earth with its fields,
> Of the first of the dust of the world.
> When he established the heavens,
> I was there,
> When he drew a circle on the face of the deep,
> When he made firm the skies above, when he established
> the fountains of the deep,

When he assigned to the sea its limit,
So that the waters might not transgress his command,
When he marked out the foundations of the earth,
Then I was beside him, like a master workman;
And I was daily his delight,
Rejoicing before him always,
Rejoicing in his inhabited world
And delighting in the sons of men.
                              (Proverbs 8: 22-31)

And what is Sophia's connection to us? Sophia is the divine feminine overshadowing Isis, Athena, Kwan Yin, Sarasvati, White Buffalo Woman, Virgin Mary, the Black Madonna and Kali just as Christ is the divine masculine overshadowing Jesus and Krishna. Just as Christ is both a key to our awakening and also an example of it, so is Sophia. Christ's path is that of love and Sophia's is that of wisdom, although love and wisdom blend into one quality on higher frequencies.

Before the advent of Christianity, Sophia, in her role of divine feminine, was regarded as the wayshower to eternal life. In Egypt as Isis, she was called the Lady of the House of Life and possessed the ankh, which was the symbol of divine authority. Speaking of herself, Isis says:

I gave and ordered laws for men, which no one is able to change...
I am she that is called goddess by women...
I divided the earth from the heaven.
I showed the paths of the stars.
I ordered the course of the sun and the moon.
I devised business in the sea.
I brought together woman and man.
I appointed to women to bring their infants to birth in the tenth month.
I ordained that parents should be loved by children.
I laid punishment upon those disposed without natural affection toward their parents.
I made with my brother Osiris an end to the eating of men.

I revealed mysteries unto men.
I taught men to honour the images of the gods....
I made the right to be stronger than gold and silver.
I ordained that the true should be thought good...
I am the Queen of rivers and sea.
No one is held in honour without my knowing it.
I am the Queen of wars.
I am the Queen of the thunderbolt.
I stir up the sea and I calm it.
I am in the rays of the sun...
I set free those in bonds...
I overcome Fate.

(Grant, Hellenistic Religions)

The time has now come for the divine feminine to descend onto the Earth to raise the planet and humanity to a higher dimension. This is prophesied in many places among which is *Revelation 12:1* in the Bible where John speaks of his vision of a woman who is with child, and who is "clothed with the sun, with the moon under her feet and on her head a crown of twelve stars." Sophia is that woman and the child is the Earth and all beings living on it. The crown of twelve stars represent twelve planets in our solar system and twelve dimensions in our consciousness. (Every decade science is discovering more dimensions and redefining our understanding of the solar system.)

In the last two thousand years humanity has focused on masculine images of the Creator and it is now time to rebalance this image to include the feminine aspect. Sophia's role in our lives will become increasingly clear in the next two thousand years. Two thousand years ago the Cosmic Christ, the Divine Son, anchored the spiritual fire of love on the Earth. Presently, Sophia, the Divine Mother and Daughter, is moving through lower frequencies to anchor the fire of spiritual wisdom onto the Earth. Sophia brings the wisdom of the stars with her over these next two thousand years. This wisdom is necessary for the Earth to become a conscious planet in our galaxy and for humanity to become conscious co-creators on this planet.

Sophia's influence, and that of the feminine principle, is re-emerging and she has appeared all over the world where she is most often referred to as The Lady. Most often these sightings appear to children, women, peasants, nuns—seldom priests or the successful. Typically she is a beautiful woman emanating blinding light. Bernadette Soubirous, who saw Sophia in Lourdes, France called the apparition Lady Aquero meaning "that one" or "her" and the lady appeared as a girl of about 14 years and not as the mother of Christ. Lucia, one of the seers in Fatima in Portugal in 1917 also called the apparition Our Lady. The Lady asked her followers to pray for peace through the Immaculate Heart of Mary. This was similar to Our Lady of all Nations that appeared in Amsterdam in 1951 and the Queen of Peace that appeared in Medjugorje in Yugoslavia in 1981. She provides healing, peace, and hope to the countless millions of pilgrims who seek her in these places. At the same time she warns us of impending disaster and encourages us to take action through our hearts both in prayer and right living. The appearances of Sophia have increased since 1830 in Europe and have in common that they look towards the end of time, as we know it, called metanoia.

In many images of Sophia she is seen as veiled because her influence is unseen and so deep in our unconscious that it is difficult to speak of her. Her work lies beneath the verbal level. In the same way that it is impossible to hold mist in your hand, it is impossible to circumscribe Sophia. Yet, as with the mist that brings needed moisture to the Earth, we see Sophia's immense impact on us and our world. The environmental movement to clean up our air and water, and to eliminate pesticides and herbicides from our soil, are under Sophia's protection. Likewise, are solar and wind power, the search for alternative renewable energy sources, and the books about consciousness in nature spirits that are increasing in popularity. That it is okay for men to cry and for women to chair boardrooms are all signs of Sophia's emergence in our world as roles of men and women dissolve to be replaced by more androgenous humans.

To discover and develop Sophia's qualities in ourselves it is helpful to examine the higher state of the feminine powers. Here we find deep faith and loyalty to the Divine, trust, compassion for those who suffer, civilization according to spiritual laws, applied wisdom, patience, tolerance, justice, knowledge of the natural world—the plant, mineral, animal kingdoms and aligning ourselves to cycles of nature in our lives. To these qualities we can add sexuality in all forms including pleasure, healing, procreation, enlightenment and sensuality—the love and expression of our senses.

The Holy Spirit

When the masculine energies of the Christ unite with the feminine energies of Sophia—meaning also, when love and wisdom unite—they birth the child of the Divine into form. Everything that is filled with spirit and consciousness in the world including people, animals, insect, trees, rocks and water are children of the Divine and are evolving in consciousness.

Spirit and matter, the masculine and feminine, Christ and Sophia are not separate and as these two balance in our personalities we move to higher frequencies where these two birth the child of unity, our true Self. During the first part of the journey the personality might erroneously believe that it must die in order to become enlightened. This is another form of dualism, as this belief values spirit above the material and ignores the fact that matter is another form of spirit. The path through the middle leads to the divine marriage of spirit and matter, the masculine and feminine, so a person is able to remain in a physical body on the Earth as a soul-infused personality.

Each of us is a child of the Creator. As children of the Divine we are the link between the spirit and the Earth and our task is to learn how to manifest spirit on the Earth. To do this, we need to understand the kundalini energy, which is the spiritual fire within us.

The Holy Spirit is another name for this kundalini energy. In each of our hearts is a flame of the three-fold aspect of divinity: will, love-wisdom, and active intelligence. This flame grows from being a one-inch flame when we are relatively unconscious to our bodies being all flame as we develop consciousness. This flame of the Holy Spirit is the same flame that descended unto the heads of the disciples of Jesus after his death so they could become teachers. It is the same flame that is shown as a halo around the heads of saints and other spiritual people. This kundalini energy gives pleasure in sex, stimulates creativity, assists in healing, and also leads to spiritual enlightenment.

Moses, the Old Testament prophet, encountered the Holy Spirit in the form of a burning bush on the top of Mt. Sinai. In the Bible we read that God spoke to him and gave him the Ten Commandments with which to lead his people into their new age. In an ancient monastery dedicated to St. Catherine at the foot of Mt. Sinai there are some of the oldest Christian paintings and texts in the world. Here, a fourth century painting shows Moses' encounter with the burning bush and the divine figure inside the bush is clearly a female, and not a male, God. This representation is aligned to the earliest Old Testament traditions where the Holy Spirit is shown as wisdom and the feminine presence of the Divine, and this spirit is sometimes seen as being synonymous with Sophia.

The sound emerging from the Holy Spirit is the universal symbol for the Creator. It is Aum in the Vedas, Hum to the Tibetans and is the origin of Amen for Christians. This sound is the frequency of creation, the heartbeat of the Earth and the basis of life for each atom. This sound frequency flows through our bodies as the kundalini energy.

The kundalini energy is how our physical bodies experience spirit. Drugs and meditation can open us to these realms of bliss and there are various levels of intensity that might occur. Some of my earliest childhood memories are of being in nature where I felt the bliss of the Holy Spirit coursing through my body as a fire of consciousness, where I and everything were One. Many children have had a similar experience but might have forgotten it, just as they forget their "imaginary" friends from other realms. The Holy Spirit has continued to bless me throughout my life and in its own time without my instigation and sometimes to my embarrassment or physical discomfort. You may have the same kind of intimate relationship with Christ or Sophia or, like me, with the Holy Spirit, and feel more drawn to either the masculine and feminine expressions of the Divine. Ultimately, these three energies are one.

Exercise 4: The Trinity in Your Life

Take a moment to still your mind before contemplating your answers to each of these questions and record your observations in your journal.

❖ In what ways do you experience the three aspects of the Divine: The Father, The Mother and The Holy Spirit?

❖ Which aspect of this Trinity do you feel the greatest affinity with and why?

❖ Which aspect do you feel drawn to incorporate now in your life? In what way?

❖ What can you do to incorporate the balance of the three aspects in your life?

Creation of Beings

We have discussed the triune-nature of the Divine, our Creator. However, we need to stretch further to see that in the universe there is more than just one Creator, and that humanity's Creator is evolving within the manifested realm. This might be a shocking concept to some but in order to understand the entire process of creation—so we humans can become full co-creators—it is essential to examine this.

When science talks about the birth of galaxies this can also be seen as the birth of Creator gods whose consciousness manifests in the third-dimensional reality that is visible to humans. Astronomers have discovered that the universe is expanding outwards and they cannot find one point for what science calls the big bang. This means that new worlds are continually being birthed out of the Void.

It is estimated that there are at least 100 billion stars in our galaxy. Within our galaxy each solar system is made up of consciously evolving beings such as our Sun and Earth. What astronomers call the Galactic Centre in the constellation of Sagittarius is the fiery heart of the Great Central Sun of our Milky Way galaxy, which is our Creator. The physical galaxy we perceive is a reflection of an invisible, multidimensional galaxy from which energy emerges from the Void into our third dimension visible dimension. This topic is examined in more detail in the chapter *The Sun* on page 167 which deals more with scientific and technical information that supports the evolution of our own solar system.

Within each individual human are the seeds that in time will make us into co-creators. We see this in the Christian story when Jesus' disciples marvelled at his miracles he replied, "And all of this and more you will do." Jesus was not engaging in flattery, but was telling the literal truth. We are evolving as our Creator continues to evolve, and even as humans in the future will evolve past what we are able to do presently. Our children inherit what we have learned. This is clearly illustrated in human evolution where we have evolved from one-celled organisms to complex beings. This process of evolution is continuous for each individual, for the collective human race, and also for the Creator.

So, like the Creator, originally we think of ourselves as a separate independent unit, while at the same time sensing, just outside our reach, that there are others. From our isolation and desire for connection, we begin to open up and move forward. This is where we start to actively grow to consciousness. We expand into our environment to find out who else is there. The first part of our learning mimics the Creator's. We expand because of our mental hunger to know, our emotional hunger to connect, and our physical hunger to be touched.

We search for the other, the part that will complete us, where we can feel the unity, the wholeness that exists in the unmanifested world of spirit. And we don't find it. Ultimately, we come back to ourselves. We turn from expanding into the macrocosm of our outside environment and contract back into the microcosm of ourselves. So our second state is contraction. This process of expansion and contraction is what the Creator did and what humans must also do in order to evolve.

When a star contracts, it appears to the human eye as if the star is dying. We know from scientific evidence that our own star, our Sun, has gone through two or more of these contractions (implosions) in its life. These implosions are the equivalent of the dark night of the soul for our Sun. The purpose of these contractions is to take what has been learned, digest it, and leave behind what is no longer needed for the next state of its evolution. This is how our Sun, humans, and the Great

Central Sun that is our Creator, evolve. Until then, the Creator was the unmanifested God the Father, Brahman, existing outside of time and space, which physicists call the no boundary condition. At the point where evolution commenced, the Creator became the second principle of God the Mother.

Every living being and race, not only in our solar system but also in our galaxy, is a cell within the body of the Creator. When the Creator contracted back into himself, into his inner core, he recognized the aliveness of each of his cells, although each cell (being) was as yet unconscious. When the Creator touched the little spark of consciousness within each of his cells the flame of yearning for more consciousness was ignited in some. Each cell was offered the opportunity to leave the unmanifested aspect of the Creator, which exists outside of time and space, in order to enter the path of evolution to become a conscious Creator. Some left, but the majority stayed. The ones who ventured forth had the greatest strength and humans were among them.

The Creator was filled with joy in being able to help others to become conscious co-creators. Humans feel this as well when we help those not as fortunate as ourselves. By watching each cell the Creator became conscious of various aspects of himself. Through struggles and gains as we evolve, we bring knowledge back to him. Each species and race has a certain unique quality because originally we came from a certain cell within the Creator. Even though each individual has all the qualities that are needed to become a conscious creator, each person still has a unique gift. Each individual must fully develop this gift to a conscious state in order to magnify the whole of creation.

Process of Expansion and Contraction

When we humans undergo a contraction, a dark night of the soul, we return to our inner core. We release our attachment to things that we wanted in the outer world: relationships, homes, security, and so on. Often contracting back into ourselves feels like a collapse, and we feel shrunken and minimized. This occurs because we enter the microcosm, the smallest parts of ourselves. We analyze our behaviours, relationships, values, health, successes and failures, everything, in fact, which gives us our identity. The process is one of letting go of learned beliefs from our parents and society. By doing this, we seek to answer the question, "Who am I?" for by knowing ourselves we discover our purpose in life. After we obtain some clarity and answers through this spiritual question, we expand back into the world to fulfil our purpose.

During our first period of expansion we most often seek teachers and others like us to answer our questions. That is because in our first period of expansion we have a desire to reproduce ourselves. This stage is exemplified by parents who wish their children to follow in their footsteps and to be like them. Our second period of expansion is very different from the first. The first expansion was more a personality need; the second, more a soul need. During the second period we desire to raise everyone and everything into consciousness based on what they need and not to prop up our own ego.

The process of expansion and contraction is how we birth ourselves. We need to expand as far as we contract. Some of us might prefer to expand while others might prefer to contract, but in harmonizing with divine law we learn to balance the two principles of expansion and contraction. We, like tides, must learn to live in the flowing and ebbing of existence. The key is not to be attached to the cycle we are in and to let it flow through us.

As well as learning the principles of expansion and contraction, we learn the balance between the two polarities. This occurs by staying in our hearts, which is the mid-point in our physical body. In our hearts we find the essence of what we were searching for all along. Now we consciously recognize the life within us which links to all other life. The qualities of love, wisdom and will, which we sought from others, reside in our hearts. Yet, paradoxically, we discover this only through the process of first seeking these qualities outside of ourselves. T. S. Eliot writes about this journey of discovery in the poem *The Four Quartets*, when he says, "…and the end of all our exploring will be to arrive where we started and know the place for the first time." This is what happens when we rise to a higher level of consciousness.

In our world we have a tendency to value the light and the period of expansion more than the dark and the period of contraction. We value the *yang* of doing and understanding more than the *yin* of being and not knowing. Just as the body must sleep at night for health, and winter allows the Earth to rest, so we must equally balance periods of expansion and contraction. Not doing so is to fear death, the dark, the feminine and ultimately the Earth. It is helpful to remember that, as in the yin-yang figure, dark always exists within the light and light always exists within the dark.

Principle of Expansion and Contraction

Expansion	Contraction
Yang	Yin
Doing	Being
Positive	Negative
Sun	Moon
Male	Female
Flow	Ebb
Manifesting	Unmanifesting
Assertion	Reflection
Life	Death

Figure 3 - The classic yin/yang figure displays the interplay of opposites in the microcosm and macrocosm of creation.

The laws of evolution create through the magnetic polarities, which are the yin/yang poles of duality. This is true at all levels of existence, as for example, in the microcosm where an atom consists of a proton, an electron and a neutron, which is the balance between the two. This is likewise true in the macrocosm where suns are like a proton and have a positive charge, and the planets are like electrons that spin around the positively charged sun. The neutral balance, which is found in higher dimensions around suns, allows travel outside of space and time and outside solar systems. It is important to note that the neutral state has a very slight positive charge of attraction that I refer to as neutral-positive, which allows movement and change between solar systems and dimensions.

This principle of the three polarities also works with humans. Our very breathing that we need to maintain life is anchored to the rhythm of expansion—breathing out—and contraction—breathing in—with a neutral pause between the two states. The positive charge expands us into the manifested world, and the negative charge contracts us into the unmanifested world of the Void. To become full co-creators we need to balance the flow of expansion with the ebb of contraction and learn how to maintain that neutral balance between the two. This neutral balance is "the still point of the turning world" of which T. S. Eliot speaks in *The Four Quartets*. The still point of the turning world is the neutral point between expansion and contraction where we balance doing and being. We need to learn to maintain a neutral-positive balance in order to become conscious co-creators. In our spiritual development, we usually learn both to expand and contract before we learn the neutral-positive point of balance between the other two.

To better understand what being in the neutral-positive state would look like in your own life, let's look at an example. Say that you have a home that you enjoy. You fix it up to look its best, however if you need to move because of a change in your work you can easily leave and create beauty in your new home. You are equally unattached to living in an apartment, a house beside water, or a house in a subdivision, although you might have an unattached preference for one of these. You can apply the neutral-positive state to every aspect of your life, such as what work you do in the world, who you are married to, and having or not having children.

The enjoyment of sexual intercourse with another is a bodily form of the expansion-contraction-neutral cycle. During sexual intercourse our hearts expand to join with the other, and our bodies follow suit. When we feel we cannot expand one iota more our bodies call for us to contract. Just before the contraction the high point of pleasure of orgasm occurs. At this point of pleasure we are in the neutral-positive state between the expansion and contraction. Contraction allows us to feed the rest of our body through our kundalini channels with the energy pleasure we had in the neutral state. Try to remember the enjoyment of orgasm when you are in your next phase of contraction, and it might lighten your spirit. The depth to which we can release is the depth to which we can expand in the next cycle. This principle applies physically, emotionally, mentally and spiritually.

Sex and procreation exist in many different forms in our universe, and fertilization occurs at the moment when expansion and contraction are balanced in the neutral-positive state. When we are fertile we can birth not only physical children, but also our ideas and thoughts—parts of ourselves—which become realities in the world. The Creator had the desire to birth parts of himself into the world, as we also do when we have children. Once again our Creator's evolution mirrors our own; the laws in our material world reflect those in higher worlds.

Exercise 5: Expansion and Contraction in Your Life

Take a moment to still your mind before contemplating your answers to each of these questions and record your observations in your journal.

❖ Which aspects of your work and personal life are in expansion?

❖ Which aspects of your work and personal life are in contraction?

❖ In what areas of your life do you feel comfortable with expansion?

❖ In what areas of your life do you feel comfortable with contraction?

❖ In what areas of your life are you able to maintain neutral-positive?

❖ In which areas of your life would you like to increase your ability to maintain neutral-positive? This is your area of growth.

Physically you might assume that people expand when they are younger and contract in later life. While this is valid, generally speaking, it is not always true. A short time ago a participants in one of my seminars said she had been a severe asthmatic, an invalid, until the age of forty. She then decided to change her belief system and now at age sixty she skis, runs, hikes and is incredibly fit. In my life I am in a period of expansion and am writing more books, doing DVDs, creating new websites and teaching more classes than I did a decade ago and, at a time, when many people of my age are retiring from work. We can also be expanding spiritually, emotionally and mentally while contracting physically. Each of us when listening to what the Divine wants of us might expand or contract in different ways and times.

Dimensions of Existence

The Creator exists in all dimensions simultaneously. So do humans since we are the very cells of the Creator. However the Creator is conscious in all dimensions, while humans, it goes without saying, are not. The Creator, the Great Central Sun, called by science our galactic centre, created a galaxy whose fundamental aspect is characterized by variable frequencies and intensities between oppositely charged poles. These variable frequencies create the twelve dimensions of existence inhabited by a multitude of evolving beings.

Twelve planes or dimensions exist simultaneously throughout the solar system and galaxy. However, that does not mean that all beings have conscious access to all twelve dimensions. The average human, for example, is conscious up to and including the third dimension. The first dimension may be viewed as a dot, the second dimension as a straight line or a flat surface, and the third dimension as a three dimensional object such as a sculpture that has height, width and depth. There are higher dimensions even than these, and physicists now accept the strong possibility of eleven dimensions. The current thought is that some of these dimensions might be very small and, like black holes, we do not see them, although their effect is felt in our 3-D world.

Science lags behind metaphysical observation because it still works with tools of the third-dimensional physical world. Nevertheless, the present is an exciting time as the knowledge of science and metaphysics starts to converge. During the next hundred years the existence of the fourth dimension will become well accepted, and science and technologies will make use of this information. During this next hundred years contact will likely be made with sentient life forms from other stars. It is important to know as much as possible about the fourth and fifth dimensions where sentient life also exists. For our discussion, we will focus on the lower five dimensions that most directly affect us while we live in physical bodies. Humans must learn the laws of these five dimensions in order to master the five levels of spiritual transformation to become conscious co-creators.

To become a co-creator we must know and be able to create with the laws of each dimension. The majority of human beings have not yet mastered the laws of the third-dimension, which they erroneously think they are conscious and awake in. True awakening occurs in much higher dimensions. And when we are able to know and rest in the fifth dimension, to a great extent we will be able to control the mind to create reality in keeping with divine laws.

Human Consciousness in Five Dimensions

Dimension	Form	Frequency /Hertz	Level of Consciousness	Issues
5th	Causal Body 'I'	Beyond speed of light	Superhuman	Thoughts create form and reality. Knowing
4th	Holographic	22-28	Astral	Maintain positive emotions Both-And thought
3rd	3-D	15-21	Animal includes ego-focused humans	Fixed physical forms Either-Or thought
2nd	Line	8-14	Plants	Giving
1st	Point	1-7	Minerals	The 7 visible and 5 invisible colours

Figure 4 - A reference chart summarizing aspects of the five dimensions of human co-creation on Earth.

The first dimension is the lowest frequency ranging on a scale from one through seven hertz. Even the first dimension is conscious, but we associate it more with the level of consciousness attained by the lower forms of the mineral kingdom. There are twelve rays of energy that bring life to the twelve dimensions. Seven of these rays are found in the seven colours of the rainbow, and five of the rays are higher frequencies of the higher dimensions. In the mineral kingdom these twelve rays are reflected as colours in gems and stones.

The second dimension is characterized by a frequency from eight to fourteen hertz. This is the level of consciousness attained by plants that interact with the Sun (the highest consciousness of our solar system) to produce life. In the second dimension humans, like plants, learn to give back what they have received from the Divine. Plants are energy donors to all beings on Earth. Individual plants work with different rays and can be used to heal deficiencies in that ray. This extensive topic can be studied more fully in herbology, homeopathy and aromatherapy.

The third dimension is the home of the animal kingdom, which also includes humans who are controlled by their animal impulses of ego craving. Here, the frequencies range from fifteen to twenty-one hertz. This energy takes the form of solidified thought. As we think something, it comes into existence. The third dimension is a plane of duality, of black and white, bad and good ways of thinking. This is the material world of the five senses exemplified by individuals who say, "If I cannot see, hear or touch something then it is not real." The third dimension has a frozen fixed nature like a sculpture.

Human beings are now at the state where they are beginning to become conscious in the fourth dimension. In order to understand the difference between the third and the fourth dimension imagine that the third dimension is like a sculpture of a seagull. The sculpture has breadth and depth, height and width, but it does not move. The fourth dimension is like a seagull in flight as seen in a movie. It has the breadth and depth, height and width of the third dimension and it also moves. It looks real, but it is an image that has the illusion of life. It is, in fact, a hologram.

When we perceive only the third dimension we are in the first and second levels of consciousness mentioned in Figure 2 on page 9. When our frequency resonates with the fourth dimension we are in third or fourth level of consciousness, which is the control of the lower and higher mental body. The fifth dimension is experienced by an individual in the fifth level of consciousness. An individual whose frequency is that of the third and fourth dimensions can fully perceive and function in the 3D material world, but an individual whose frequency is that of the third dimensional world cannot perceive the higher dimensions.

Our entire reality, our physical world and all that is in it, including our physical image of ourselves, are like holograms, three dimensional objects which are able to move in the space and time dimension. The ancient Vedic scriptures state that we are a dream being dreamt by God. Not only is God dreaming us into existence, we are thinking our own world into existence. We are creating our own reality. This can be a frightening thought for many people, and is no doubt the reason why this knowledge is not part of our everyday reality. Once we realize that our mind creates our reality, we must take total responsibility for our behaviours, our health, our environment—the list goes on. How many of us want to do that? It's much easier to cling to the thought that we are the victims of outside forces beyond our control. However, once we start living and working consciously in the fourth dimension, as many of us are starting to do now, we realize this to be true.

Einstein was a pioneer in speaking of the existence of a fourth dimension, which he said allowed us to travel to the past and future. Paramahansa Yogananda in his book, *The Divine Romance*, says, "The fourth dimension is the sphere of lifetrons, which can be perceived only through the sixth sense of intuition." These *lifetrons* are the same as the *prana* of which Hindu scriptures speak. Prana is intelligent, alive and finer than atomic matter. The fourth dimension is the astral world, what we think of as heaven and hell in the Judeo-Christian tradition. We experience this dimension after death, and can also experience this realm consciously when we raise our frequency.

The astral world of the fourth dimension is populated by disembodied souls who are between incarnations. This dimension is very challenging as it is fuelled by emotions where battles rage between our personality and our higher Self. It is in this realm where the battle that Christians refer to as Armageddon is currently being fought. Sometimes people dream about this, for dreams occur in the astral plane. The fourth dimension is the gateway to higher worlds. The way to progress above the fourth dimension is through overcoming duality and learning to forgive others and ourselves.

The fourth dimension has positive aspects as well. Individuals might have psychic or mystical experiences, talk with spirit guides and channel information from various masters. These can be fourth dimensional experiences that contain conditional truths, which help strengthen people's spiritual commitment. As our negativity and fears are purified and transmuted, our soul merges with our personality vessel. Humanity will likely pass through this dimension within this next two thousand year period and enter the fifth dimension.

Because our Earth is currently moving to the fourth dimension in its consciousness it also is undergoing much purification, a healing crisis in the third dimension of her physical body, which takes the form of volcanoes, hurricanes, and global warming. A magnetic pole reversal, which could happen at any time, will signal her movement into the fourth dimension. Individuals who have been purifying their astral, etheric and physical bodies will be able to move into the fourth dimension with the Earth. Those who have not will find themselves in a very unpleasant third dimensional level of existence on the Earth. If they so choose, the opportunity is available for them to raise their frequency so they can enter higher dimensions.

Those individuals who have already worked on purifying and stabilizing their emotions will be able to go to the fifth dimension during the Earth's rise to the fourth dimension. However, some of these individuals might voluntarily decide to remain in the third or fourth dimensions to assist others in their purification and rise to consciousness.

On entering the fifth dimension our entire view of reality changes, and we *know* that we are part of everything else. Although we might encounter Christ, Buddha or other Masters who are overseeing our evolution, we know that they and we are all aspects of the same Divine Spirit. In the fifth dimension we learn to consciously create form with our mind and communication with humans and other beings will be through telepathy. In the fifth dimension we will be able to use our higher senses of sight, hearing, touch, taste, smell as well as intuition to know what another being needs from us and, because love will be experienced as the essential law, we will give freely. The fifth dimension is one of peace, harmony and oneness with all living beings.

The frequencies in this fifth dimension are beyond the speed of light. In Hindu texts this is referred to as the causal world or world of thoughts. Whatever we can do physically at present, we will be able to do with our thoughts in the future. There are, of course, evolved humans who can do this even now while still in a human form.

There are higher dimensions of consciousness than these five and some enlightened humans exist in these levels, however it is difficult to maintain a physical body in the third dimension if our consciousness is higher than the fifth dimension. This is because the difference in frequencies is too great.

So how can you use this information in your life? The first thing I is to focus on the issues in front of you now, because as you solve those you will naturally move to a higher dimension. The second thing is to enjoy the beauty of all the dimensions and not to feel inadequate if you rest most of the time in the third dimension. For example, I love plants and gardening, which links me to the second and third dimension, and I spend many happy hours in my garden pruning, weeding and celebrating the beauty of nature.

Exercise 6:
Developing Consciousness in Five Dimensions

Take a moment to still your mind before contemplating your answers to these questions. Referring to Figure 4 on page 35 review the five dimensions to develop your consciousness in each of these levels. In the next five days contemplate your relationships in these dimensions and at the end of the day write your reflections in your journal.

❖ Day One: Dedicate to the first dimension to develop your consciousness in the mineral kingdom with emphasis on the colours OR, if you prefer, examine your relationship with each of the colours of the rainbow.

❖ Day Two: Dedicate to the second dimension to develop your consciousness in the plant kingdom with emphasis on giving. Examine the ways in which plants give to you and practice selfless giving.

❖ Day Three: Dedicate to the third dimension to develop your consciousness in the animal kingdom with emphasis on societies' rules and roles. Examine the ways in which you live your life according to roles and rules.

❖ Day Four: Dedicate to the fourth dimension to develop your consciousness in the astral dimension with emphasis on maintaining positive emotions and forgiving yourself and others.

❖ Day Five: Dedicate to the fifth dimension with emphasis on unconditional love and using your intuition to know what others need from you.

Creating in Time and Space

There are twelve dimensions in our galaxy and each human being has twelve bodies (four of which are the physical, etheric, emotional and mental) that mirror this pattern. These twelve bodies are energy fields created by thought located in the ethers, which form vortexes, or wheels, called *chakras*, that build and feed these bodies. (An overview of the first seven chakras is given on page 76).

Seven of the twelve chakras expand through mini-wormholes— approximately 10-33 cm in diameter according to physicist Jack Saratti—into worlds of form while five of these chakras contract trough these mini-wormholes into the Void of subspace. These wormholes are beyond space and time and connect every point in space to every other point in space throughout the universe. We manifest our thoughts and dreams through the seven chakras into the world and de-manifest what we no longer need or want through the five chakras into the Void. Each of our thoughts resonates at a certain frequency. Thoughts of material pleasure activate the lower chakras, while thoughts of unconditional love and service to others activate higher chakras.

The soul, dwelling more fully in the seventh chakra because of its higher frequency, lives in space outside of chronos, or clock time. It sees the past, present and future *simultaneously*. Descending into the sixth chakra and working with the personality, the soul can choose to move forward or backward in time and space. Only the personality— anchored in chronos time as it is—sees time as linear, with the past behind and the future ahead. In order to effectively work with both the soul and personality we need to combine the space (soul) dimension with the time (personality) dimension of the material world. The more that we are open in both our seventh, sixth, fifth and fourth chakras the more that we can see, create, and manifest in both space and time.

I have found the symbol of the Celtic Cross very helpful in ascertaining how best to move in time and space. The Celtic Cross has the horizontal axis that represents time, the vertical axis that represents space, and a circle of energy that is created in the center where time and space meet.

The vertical axis of the Celtic Cross represents space. Unlimited possibilities and potential exist in the higher realms of space. As we develop our spiritual abilities, we have increasing access to these realms and are able to bring those possibilities into our physical world. It is along the vertical line that we also anchor spiritual energies to the Earth and transform the earthly energies into spirit.

On the vertical axis of the Celtic Cross we learn to purify all of our chakras so we can resonate in all frequencies, tuning our bodies like the wonderful instrument it is, to play beautiful music in all the dimensions. Such purification is accepted wisdom in many traditions ranging from the sevenfold descent of Inanna, the Sumerian goddess, to the Greek legend of Psyche, the soul, who passed through seven levels of experience to reunite with Eros. In Christianity it is the story of Mary Magdalene, the woman from whom Jesus cast out seven demons. Sophia is also associated with seven pillars and seven veils. These stories from many traditions illustrate the necessity of purifying each of the chakras in order to rise to higher frequencies and dimensions.

Creating in Time and Space

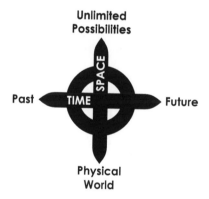

Figure 5 - Living and co-creating within the circle of time and space.

On the horizontal arm of the Celtic Cross we have time and the progression of evolution as we move from the past to the present and into the future. Within the first, second, and third dimensions we are constrained by the laws of evolution. When we rise to the fourth chakra, at the heart, where the axis of space meets the axis of time, we learn how to live and act freely in either the lower or higher dimensions. This rising to the fourth chakra necessitates a quantum leap in consciousness and one that humanity is engaging in at this moment.

Within our heart lies the still point, the neutral-positive place of rebirth into our higher self, which is the union of the soul-infused personality. We wait in non-attachment, co-operating with the transformation as best we can by meeting life's inner and outer challenges. We trust in the process and daily celebrate life with gratitude and joy. The path is simple and profound.

Living within the circle of time and space means living in the flow of the present moment. We enjoy the quality of the moment knowing that there will be enough time to do everything of importance, and we create a space for the universe to surprise us. When we live only in the physical world, we are so full of doing that we have no space left for unknown gifts. By living and working in the point of the present moment, we do and be simultaneously. We do not push against closed doors but wait for the doors to open of their own accord, and if they don't we move on to another door.

Let us examine this concept in more depth. In the third dimension in which we consciously live, there is a current of time going from the past to the future. Individual and collective past events are captured in our memories and the memories of our planet. These memories are known as the noosphere by Teilhard de Chardin, the morphogenetic field by Rupert Sheldrake, the Akashic Records in the Vedas, and the collective unconscious by C. J. Jung.

This soul realm of the collective holds archetypal images that influence humanity's evolution. These images reflect qualities that both individuals and humanity are developing or have developed. Because of the strength of past programs, developed through the feedback loop of individuals over millennia telling the stories and emulating the characters, the old patterns of the personality are reinforced. Presently these archetypes are strengthened through television and film. Sophia and those who oversee our evolution are continually generating new archetypes, or evolving the old ones, such as Zeus and Hera of Greek myth, to higher frequencies that pull us toward the future. We must look to see what qualities Sophia is broadcasting from these up-to-date archetypes currently.

Our personality feels more comfortable with the known of the past, which is on the horizontal axis, or the lower three chakras, found on the lower part of the vertical axis. Soul and spirit more often come towards us from the future on the horizontal axis or higher realms on the vertical axis. The currents where the past of the personality and future of the soul meet are in the present moment in the body. By staying in the present moment in the body we can understand what our soul wishes our personality to do. Thus, we experience embodied and ensouled consciousness in the world as a soul-infused personality.

On the vertical axis we experience spirit and soul as being somehow above us, a potential for development that calls us to higher and nobler aspects of ourselves. Our body when firmly anchored to the Earth, is where we have the opportunity to act in ways to benefit others, the world and ourselves.

The horizontal axis of time and the vertical axis of space come together in the present moment. The body and the higher self meet the physical Earth and its Soul in this same place on the vertical axis. These four conjunctions can only be possible if we live fully in the present moment. Because these vertical and horizontal energies are not only in the third dimensional reality, when they are balanced we are able to simultaneously access multidimensions, both in and beyond space and time.

Individually and collectively, our memories from the past create the holographic image of our body and personality. By changing our thoughts, our image of ourselves and the world, and by empowering these thoughts with strong positive feelings we can transform.

To awaken from this third dimensional dream that we think is reality, we have to build up self-confidence and will power to break through the collective hypnosis of our world. First we need to be able to conceive of a different reality than the one we have currently. We need to believe that it is possible to have a world at peace, with clean air, soil, and water, where each person is seen as valuable, indeed profoundly essential to the whole of creation. We need to believe that we are needed just as we are, that no faults from the past cling to us, and that we have total freedom to be the best we can be in this very moment. And we need to see that every person who dreams this new dream strengthens the etheric body of the Earth and changes the archetypes that work with us. These dreams then become our physical reality.

The etheric, or subtle body, also called *pranamayakosa* in Tibetan Buddhism, can change the entire blueprint of who we are, awakening us to new realities. It is the memory body, not just of the past, but also of the future, not just of the physical, but also of the psychological and spiritual, not just of the waking state, but also of the dream state. Nothing is forgotten in the etheric body, although it may not be accessible to us consciously. Because dreams cross into the etheric and physical body the soul can actually nudge the ego to act in a different way. Dreams imprint us and the feelings that are elicited in the dreams energize this imprintation process.

Even if we do not do anything differently, the soul employs dreams, imagination, and intuitions to build up energy in the etheric and physical bodies that move us into action in the world. Because our energy and frequency has changed, this very change necessitates a change also in the opportunities that open to us and the situations we magnetize to us.

The key to all this happening is our heart. Love is food for the heart. People who love deeply radiate this quality and others are attracted to them for this food. For the heart, love, wisdom and action are the same. Being and doing become synonymous as we respond to what is needed. We need to keep the heart open to engage with everything and everyone in a non-attached way, including difficulties as well as joys. This occurs when people live in the present moment, open to knowledge of the past and the call from the future.

The higher expression of love is not sentimental, nor attached. We unconditionally wish the best for another person even if we cannot see what is best for that person at the time. How could we, when we ourselves are changing through unknown ways daily? We can, however, wish for the person the strength to commit to the journey and in this all else will be given. It is the same in relationship with a partner. It used to be that we thought we had to fall in love in order to commit to a person. It is possible instead to commit to loving and the journey that this love takes us on. The former is a journey of fantasy and karma; the later the journey of co-creation and transformation.

The most important question is not what do I, the little me, want?

It is what does the Spirit and the Earth, my divine and natural mothers, want of me? The people and opportunities put in my path are there for a reason. Why seek something else, to change what is? Instead, learn to deeply love what is. In this way love is freed and transformed into the gold of its highest element. Intimacy now exists on the plane of the world, not removed from it into a sphere that serves just the two people.

To love and deeply know ourselves we need a strong personality, not to be egoistic, but to have the courage and will to open to our soul in order to serve the world in whatever capacity our gifts and destiny determine. Too much spiritual work takes us out of the body and the world; too much inner work examining ourselves builds narcissism. In the uniqueness of our individuality we discover our higher self, and it is found through our evolutionary development as a human being. This is the path of love, wisdom and will, not in service to ourselves, but to the world and to spirit.

We are in our higher self when we feel as one with the world, in unity with all other beings, rocks, animals, plants, and nature, as well as all other humans. Our soul, the higher self, feels the rhythms and cycles of nature, of light and dark, birth and death, in a stream of wholeness, and it deeply accepts and feels the rightness of these. Simultaneously, the higher self feels its own purpose in this plan and moves with it in service and commitment. It flows from day to day in the stream of evolution dedicating its actions to the actions at hand with no resistance and no clutching. It knows that everything, including itself, is in continual change. It allows itself to flow with deeper and deeper levels of transformation as they present themselves. Small and great deeds are weighted the same, as all actions and non-actions find balance within the stream of evolution.

This is not to say that the path to higher consciousness is a painless experience. It might very well be more uncomfortable and difficult than the previous life of acceptance of society's norms. However, there is a deep-felt experience of rightness that comes with this choice, which in turn increases ones own joy and inner peace.

Let us ask for grace, another name for Sophia, to enter us through the dark and light times equally. Our duty is to go on our own journey, which by necessity involves evolving truth. People may come and go in our life on this journey. Bless those that go, bless those that stay, and know that cycles return like the ebb and flow of the oceans, the inbreath and outbreath of creation.

In the *Gnostic Gospel of Eve*, Sophia says:

> It is I who am you, and it is you who are me.
> And wherever you are, I am there.
> And I am sown in all; and you collect me from wherever you wish.
> And while you collect me, it is your own self that you collect.

I'd like to share with you an example from my own life using the model of creating in time and space. When I was writing *Take Your Soul to Work* I found myself wondering from time to time who would publish the book. No answer came forth and so I did not push it but continued to stay open to the universe's suggestions.

I had just finished the book and was on a plane reading a flight magazine. In it was an article on the ten most eligible bachelors in Canada. Being single at the time I decided to read about them. One stood out. He was the head of Canada's largest publishing house and in the article he said, "I love my work so much that I would do it even if it didn't pay me." His attitude was the theme of *Take Your Soul to Work* and the lights started flashing. I wrote him a letter telling him the synchronicity and received a telephone call a few weeks later asking for the manuscript. The book had found its publisher.

I am going to suggest an exercise for creating in time and space. Doing this exercise moves you into your heart where both your personal will and divine will meet. From this place in your heart you will be open to both give and receive and your highest destiny will come to you.

Evolution of the Angels

As we progress on our spiritual path we begin to suspect that humans are not the only conscious beings. When we begin to move into the fourth and fifth dimensions, this suspicion becomes reality.

From the beginning of humanity's recorded history there have been references to angels. There are angels in Zoroastrianism, Buddhism, Taoism as well as Judaism, Christianity and Islam. There are thousands of books devoted to the study of angels including many that contain stories of personal encounters from such diverse people as Johnny Cash, George Washington, Albert Einstein, Goethe, Rudolph Steiner and Black Elk.

During the last thirty or forty years angels have become mainstream and many movies have been made involving accounts of angels. In the 1990's *Time* magazine conducted a poll to find out how many people believed in angels. The respondents were members of various religious traditions, and of no religious tradition, and yet a majority of them believed in angels. Many people trust angels, when they might not trust spirit guides, animal totems, past life regressions and a multitude of gateways into the spirit world. In fact, for many, angels are their only connection with the world of spirit and are the beings who lift them into higher states of consciousness. So let's examine the function of angels in our lives.

The word angel in Greek means *messenger* and angels are messengers of the Divine. Angels are the essence of the consciousness that we refer to as the Creator and they feed us whether we are consciously aware of them or not. There are guardian angels who stay with us our entire life and these angels assist us with our purpose in this life. They continually strengthen the specific quality that will ensure success in our task. Angels have different qualities and our guardian angel could gift us specifically with healing, forgiveness, hope, patience, or whatever we need. Other angels might help us at various times in our life when we need a specific quality that they have. If, for example, we have just lost a loved one and pray to God for help, an angel of peace might send us this quality of energy so that we are consoled.

Dionysius, an early Christian scholar, wrote *De Hierarchia Celesti* around 500 AD in which he grouped angelic beings into various types. Many other spiritual writers, including the Austrian mystic Rudolph Steiner, have also accepted these categories. I list these types so you can have an idea of the broad range of functions performed by angels. At the top of the hierarchy are Seraphim who receive the ideas and aims of the cosmic system from the Holy Trinity. Cherubim, the second type, transpose these ideas into workable human plans. The Thrones, the third level down, work with humans to put the thoughts received from the Seraphim into practice. The next grouping of angelic beings include Dominions, Mights-Virtues and Powers who, as Dionysius says, work to regulate angelic duties, miracles and prevent the overthrow of good in the world.

The last, and lowest category in this hierarchy, includes Archangels and Angels. Archangels govern the relationship between individual human beings and their specific race, as well as the human race in general. From the Judaic tradition we learn the names of four great Archangels who have had significant contact with humanity. The first of these, Michael, whose name means *looks like God*, is God's defender. The second is Gabriel, meaning *faithful spirit and hero of God*, who is associated with the annunciation of Mary and connected with judgment and mercy. Third is Uriel, meaning *light of God*, an interpreter of prophesies and associated with divine knowledge. The fourth is Raphael *divine healer*, who watches over all humanity.

Some individuals have had contact with the great archangels, but more often people have contact with lesser angels. Angels have been described variously as radiant light, floating in the air, with or without wings, and sometimes looking like ordinary humans. Some individuals have seen angels with their eyes; others have felt them as invisible helpers. For example, explorer Sir Ernest Shackleton and his crew reported that, during his shipwreck and life threatening return from the South Pole, they were accompanied by "one more."

To understand the function of angels it is helpful to examine their origin. Angels are like the blood in the Creator's body. Until the time in evolution when the Creator's consciousness contracted and went inward, angels performed their function instinctively in accord with Spirit. Angels do not have free will and do not question their function; they go and do whatever the Creator wants. Angels are totally dedicated to the first commandment in the Bible, which is "to love thy God with all thy heart." Angels experience no doubt, no lack of faith. They are the essence of the Divine, just as other races, such as humans, represent different functions in the divine body. When the Creator birthed the various races he did not want them to have to struggle alone. So he sent forth his blood, the angels, to infuse them, watch over them, strengthen them and be like blood brothers to them.

Early in evolution the Creator offered the great angels an opportunity to incarnate into some races to learn the use of free will. Their motivation for incarnating was so they could be of more use to the Creator. In selfless dedication the archangels left their original status, to which they were totally committed, and devoted millions of years learning the principles of creation, so they would be able to birth other angels to help evolving beings.

Some of the great angels entered these evolutions for a limited time for this experience. Doing so benefited both the angels and the various sentient beings that they entered because the beings were infused with the essence that these angels brought. This was like a blood transfusion and both angels and the other beings grew from and were changed by this experience. Through this process some angels became hybrids. They were no longer pure angels as they had mixed their essence with that of other beings, including the human.

The archangels can birth minor angels, just as the Creator did with them. To do this, they breathe forth their essence and create minor versions of themselves. To understand this concept imagine Russian dolls, where you look inside one and there is another one, smaller and yet identical to the larger doll. Like those dolls, the minor angels are all perfect representations of the greater angels, just smaller in size and in energy. Smaller angels have neither free will, nor their own individuality, nor do they want it.

There are various types of angels. Each type embodies a specific quality and is able to strike a certain note such as peace, hope, healing, and love. The note of hope, for example, will be the same note of hope from a young or an older angel. The only difference is the young angel does not have the same power as the older one to change the frequency of the person they are assisting. Also, the depth to which the frequency can penetrate through dimensions and the strength of that call will be greater for the greater angels. This is similar to the fact that a larger bell can strike a stronger note than a smaller one and can be heard further away by more people.

Long before humanity's beginnings archangels entered evolutions of earlier beings. They did this in higher dimensions. Having completed this evolution, these great angels renewed their dedication and sacrificed their free will once again to the Creator's will. Within angelic realms this is the equivalent of what Jesus the Christ did on the cross when he sacrificed himself for the good of others. Not all angels developed free will, and only the Great Ones are being referred to here.

Archangel Michael is a guardian angel on the first ray of divine will and many people who are bringing light into dark places or who are pioneers in their areas of work have told me that he helps them. I've also found that children are drawn to him as their protector. I would like to share with you an exercise that I have given children and adults, an exercise that I also use before sleeping to protect my body while I leave it to do other work.

Exercise 8:
Visualization for Protection by Archangel Michael

Take a moment to still your mind before doing this guided visualization.

Visualize Archangel Michael with a sword of blue flame. Visualize yourself being protected as you say these words to yourself or aloud.

- ❖ Archangel Michael, please come with your sword of blue flame and seal me in front, behind, on either side, in front and behind from everything not of the light. Seal, seal, seal.

- ❖ We may feel drawn to both Archangel Michael as well as having our own personal guardian angel. For example, your personal guardian angel might be helping you to develop love or healing whereas Archangel Michael offers you protection in your entire life.

Virgin Mary of the Christian tradition is of angelic evolution. She is the equivalent of a Master in our human evolution. A Master is a name given to someone who transcends the form of the lower five dimensions, dissolves the ego, and unites consciously with the one Spirit. Jesus demonstrated this principle physically in his ascension, although individuals may not need to physically die in order for the transformation to occur. In Jesus two evolutions mingled. The first is the angelic through his mother Mary, who as an angel carried the blood of the Creator. The second is human evolution, as Jesus was descended from the first man Adam, who is the prototype of the first human. Jesus was a hybrid in that his physical bodies were created from human genes and his spiritual essence came from angelic evolution.

In fact, many humans are hybrids. Just as humans are experimenting currently with genetic manipulation and the creation of new species, the Creator also does this. Some humans are originally of angelic evolution and there are characteristics which might be helpful in identifying them. They focus primarily on serving the Divine regardless of the religious tradition to which they adhere. Purity, in the broad sense, is often associated with humans who have angelic blood. They might appear noble or trustworthy. They might also have qualities of healing and peace, which attract people to them. This is not to say that human-angelic hybrids are perfect, as they are not.

Exercise 9: Meet Your Guardian Angel

Take a moment to still your mind before doing the following visualization. You may want to read the questions before starting, or record yourself reading the questions and then play them back, or enlist a friend to read them to you.

Everyone has a guardian angel and you can meet yours. ...Go to a private, quiet place and close your eyes....Imagine that you are in the clouds, the natural realm of the angels and that you are asking your guardian angel to make itself visible to you...(Pause between questions and give yourself time to receive answers)

- ❖ Notice a angel coming towards you and do not have preconceptions about how it should or should not look....
- ❖ How is this angel dressed? Is it more male or female in appearance?
- ❖ Is there a colour associated with this being?
- ❖ Ask this angel for its name.
- ❖ What is its role in your life?
- ❖ Is there any other question that you wish to ask?
- ❖ Does the angel want to say something to you?
- ❖ Thank the angel for coming and ask how and when you can speak with it again?

Remember all that you learned in this visualization. Take a moment to reflect on the answers before opening your eyes and record what you learned in your journal.

Lucifer and Archangel Michael

When the majority of the angels returned to the Creator's heart, some stayed apart in order to learn more. This happened before humans started their evolution. Knowledge was their great temptation. This is why in the Biblical story of the Garden of Eden the tree of knowledge was forbidden. To eat of it was to fall out of union with Divine Spirit into the lower dimensions of the mind. Archangel Lucifer was the most famous of the fallen angels and this is why he is equated with the snake of temptation in the Bible.

With the religious and cultural programming most Westerners have undergone, it is difficult to discuss Lucifer without them experiencing a negative reaction. There are several reasons for this. One is a denial of our own dark side and the wish to blame others for it. The second is a simplistic desire to divide the world into good and evil, right and wrong and to cling to what we have been taught in our western upbringing is good because it is safe. It is time to uproot this fear and examine Lucifer's function in accordance with the spiritual teachings of the Book of Life. Lucifer's story is in many ways closer to humanity's than that of Jesus. One of the great challenges on our path to consciousness is to be able to understand Lucifer's full significance in our lives.

It is commonly accepted that the name Luc-i-fer means light bringer, but it means both this and more. *Luc* is light, but *fer* is also associated with the development of iron *fer*, and with fire and boiling *fervere* and wildness *ferus*. He is the one who catalyzes humanity's development. Our quest for knowledge, like Lucifer's, initially takes us away from Spirit. This process is necessary if we are to learn wisdom, which is the higher function of knowledge.

Let's examine his story to see how it mirrors our own. Lucifer and a few other great angels, having been given free will, decided to keep it, to act with it and not to rededicate it to the whole. Lucifer was the first of the Great Ones to descend into matter and his descent was a shock in higher dimensions, which resounds even now in our stories and collective unconscious. Before Lucifer, none had rebelled against the dictates of the Creator, or had thought to do other than the his will. When Lucifer fell a wound of possibilities and uncertainties opened in the galaxy—which is the Creator's body—where, before then, there were only certainties.

Lucifer started a pattern in the macrocosm, which is reiterated in Jesus' life with Judas, and in each of our lives as we confront our own inner betrayer. Each of us has a betrayer, which is a part of ourselves that would lead us away from the light of spirit. Often during our spiritual journey we encounter an outer betrayer who falsely accuses us. It is too simplistic to say that this individual is evil and that we are the good ones. On a spiritual level, this person is doing his or her job. This betrayer might act consciously or unconsciously, but according to divine law we are tested to see if we will totally commit to serve the will of the Divine, whether we are physically killed or our reputations ruined.

Lucifer is known in many traditions outside of Christianity. To understand Lucifer's function more clearly it can be helpful to examine his role in some of these other cultures. In ancient Egypt he was known as Set. When someone died, Thoth the God of knowledge assessed his life. If the individual had not accomplished his purpose, he was condemned to the Egyptian underworld ruled by Set. In ancient Egypt Set was not considered as evil, but as fulfilling his function. Set and Lucifer's purpose is to help us to build an ego, an individual personality. On one level, this is a fall away from the Divine, which for us is the loss of our blissful state of innocence. On another level, it represents an evolutionary step. To develop consciousness we struggle back to our initial place, where we are tested to see if the material world still tempts us. Lucifer and Set's function on behalf of the Divine is to make us strong enough to become co-creators. We do not become co-creators by having an easy time, but through enduring and overcoming hardships.

Let's examine Lucifer's function in another spiritual tradition. In Tibetan Buddhism there are two teaching styles. One is kind, gentle and helpful. The other is stern, demanding and capable of causing the student much distress. The first style helps the student to expand and open to give and receive love. The second causes the student to contract and strengthen so that he or she is able to love even in adversity. Sometimes a teacher serves both functions at different times with a student. Both functions are necessary to help the student learn these two principles, and Lucifer works with the strengthening function.

In Tibetan Buddhism, Lucifer, in his guise as Heruka, is the Buddha on the southern path, the path of blood, who holds the skull and is therefore the death bringer to humanity's innocence. Heruka, the consort of Vajrayogini, is the god of the tantric path that serves the strengthening function. He wears a tiger skin loincloth and carries skulls in his hands representing the demons he has defeated. These demons represent the internal demons that each of us must defeat. Lucifer, like Heruka, is a teacher. He presents us with all the temptations of the material world, and we must refuse him during our spiritual journey. He is doing a job like the difficult teachers in many spiritual traditions who purposefully make our lives miserable in order to move us to consciousness.

Furthermore, to think that Lucifer is forever fallen is to negate the possibility of our own redemption. Lucifer guards the doors to the Void and to the collective unconscious. Whether we are aware of it or not, he will test us at the same time as we start consciously to access the collective unconscious of humanity. During this stage we question everything we have learned in order to discover higher truths, which we would not have been able to face before then. There is *not* just one truth. Truth, like everything else, evolves as we journey to consciousness. There are collective thoughtforms of Lucifer just as there are of God—you remember the old guy with the white beard— and we must transmute these outdated thoughtforms to learn the next level of truth about him.

We discover that Lucifer is no longer fallen. He has been redeemed for aeons of time through wisdom, which is the conquering of knowledge. He fell lowest, so he has suffered more pain than any other being. Here is a deeper interpretation of the biblical story of the prodigal son. Lucifer is the prodigal son of the Creator who had everything and was loved by the father. After the son, Lucifer, left the Creator he experienced much pain and hardship. On the son's return the father prepared a great feast in celebration. His other sons, who had loyally stayed with him, were envious. In the same way, when Lucifer returned to the Creator many angels questioned, "Why should Lucifer, who has done so many bad things, be so loved?" The answer is important. Lucifer left with his free will and returned with his free will. And greater was the decision to return than to leave, and greater was his strength when he decided. Lucifer gave back all he had learned to the Creator who then knew what evil was. With this knowing came more compassion and forgiveness.

What happens in the macrocosm is often mirrored in the microcosm of humanity's stories and myths. Even in our individual development, we go through a time of being when we see people in absolute terms of either being like us and good, or different than us and therefore bad. Those categorized as bad, we tend to see as a threat and enemy.

As we progress spiritually, we see the complexities in each person and treat each one differently according to his or her needs. If people do not live in accordance with divine law, we forgive them, and forgive them, and forgive them, and never give up hoping that one day they'll change. Mind you, sometimes this change does not occur in one lifetime unless, like Paul on the road to Damascus, we have a revelation and see the error of our ways.

Lucifer's story is important in our realization of consciousness. We, like Lucifer, have left higher spiritual realms, which is necessary in order to learn to use our free will. Just as teenagers need to leave their parents in order to mature, humans needed to leave the Creator in order to become Creators. It is only after we grow up and have suffered many losses and difficulties ourselves that we learn compassion and wisdom. We are humbled and now ready to return to the one who created us, our Mother-Father Creator. When we return we are greater than when we left to start our journey. This is the process of spiritual transformation.

Although Lucifer has been redeemed for millions upon millions of years, the knowledge of his redemption has not filtered down through the various dimensions of existence to become apparent in the third dimension of human consciousness. This knowledge is gradually getting closer to the third dimension and will be part of the knowledge remembered during the next two thousand years in what is referred to as the Aquarian Age. This knowledge is necessary if we are to completely understand the law of transmuting what is not of the light to the light, and vice versa.

Humanity has long suspected Lucifer of evil. He has been represented as a dragon and as Satan with horns, hooves and tail. These two evolving species affect humanity and will be addressed later. Lucifer, however, is neither of these evolutions. He is a gigantic and great being of angelic evolution. Few have seen Lucifer before their entry into the fourth and fifth dimensions, and some individuals have encountered him in their dream state. Lucifer and the angels under him are in charge of clearing our astral body as we humans move through the fourth dimension. He rests behind the veil that separates our conscious reality from the Void.

Archangel Michael and Lucifer are fraternal twins with strengths on opposite polarities, and each wields power in the visible world in a different age. These ages are very long, and Michael has ruled now in the light of day for eons. Lucifer's time to rule approaches. Humanity fears night and death and thus fears the coming of Lucifer's reign. There is no more to be feared than the present astrological change from the Piscean to the Aquarian Age. These minor changes of ages occur every two thousand years and are governed by the change in the astrological zodiac. The minor cycles occur hundreds of times more frequently than the changeover from Michael's day to Lucifer's night, and these minor cycles happen within this greater cycle.

Our world is presently undergoing one of these minor Luciferian cycles. We are entering a period of cleansing by fire of which the Hopi speak. In the Hindu tradition this period is called the Kaliyuga, so called because the goddess Kali births her children and then eats them. She is a death bringer like Lucifer, but both of them kill only what is not aligned to spiritual laws. This might take place in the outer world, as we saw during September 11, 2001 as well as the economic and environmental upsets of these last years. The changes also might take place in the inner world of our unconscious. But there is no doubt that we are presently engaged in a period of separating the wheat from the chaff. We would be encouraged to do this for ourselves lest Lucifer and other beings decide to help us.

In the macrocosm of the cosmos Lucifer's time arrives when each planet is absorbed into its sun, when the solar suns are reabsorbed into the galactic suns, when anti-matter replaces matter. This occurs in both the macrocosm and microcosm when the inner replaces the outer and inhalation replaces exhalation. This cycle is continually happening in all worlds and dimensions. Lucifer's time arrives for individuals when they enter the Void in themselves. This occurs when they enter the astral and causal dimensions.

Archangel Michael and Lucifer are brothers. They can be seen as the yang and the yin in one egg. Michael, as the yang, takes care of the outer world, and Lucifer, as the yin, takes care of the inner world. Michael guards the Sun aspect in all beings and on all levels in our solar system. Lucifer guards the Void, the ether that lies between matter. The Void contains the potential for all ideas, feelings and things that we bring into existence. When we are born our bodies are birthed from the Void. When we die we return to the Void where our bodies are de-manifested.

There is a Void in all things, from the black holes, which have once been great suns, to the Voids that exist in tiny cells. We know through science that we are made up of 99.9 percent ether. This is Lucifer's domain. We are filled as much by Lucifer, as by Michael. Michael and Lucifer work respectively with matter and antimatter, positive and negative magnetic forces. Our physical world, planet, solar system and even humans are created by balancing these two forces.

In his left hand Lucifer carries a golden ball symbolizing the egg of all formed matter. In his right hand he carries a sceptre with the cross symbolizing his power over matter. Lucifer's power is to make matter desirable to us, whereas Michael carries a sword in his right hand to symbolize his power to cut us free from that attraction to matter. It is necessary to learn how to do both functions if we are to become conscious co-creators.

Lucifer was called the Son of the Morning, or the Prince of the Morning, because he existed in the Creator's youth. He is represented wearing a six-pointed crown on his head, because at that time when Lucifer was the Prince of the Morning, there were six, not seven, chakras. When Lucifer fell there was no crown chakra—representing enlightenment—because there was no ascension as no being had fallen. At that time there was no ego, no individuals who thought of themselves as separate from the Creator. Lucifer, in his fall and in his redemption—which is the ascension, awakening, enlightenment—is the pathfinder for us.

Most humans have chosen the path of knowledge, like Lucifer, in order to become conscious co-creators. Because he was, and is, a teacher and wayshower on this path, Lucifer has been blamed for humanity's loss of Eden, the bliss realms of Spirit. The first part of the path of knowledge entails a descent into lower frequencies. Originally these frequencies consisted of only heavier material forms. However, over the millions of years of human evolution, lower frequencies have come to hold all the negative thoughts, feelings and deeds that humans have perpetrated on this planet. We are now at a collective turning point in our evolution where we are passing the darkest point and commencing our climb back into higher frequencies. We, like Lucifer, are bringing the knowledge we have acquired in our fall back to the Creator who, in turn, will increase the consciousness of the galaxy. This path of wisdom is the evolutionary path of spiritual transformation.

With wisdom we sift through and digest the pieces of knowledge that we have acquired. During this process it is necessary to face everything in ourselves that is not of the light and examine it, admit it, transmute it. We go into our own Void to clear away all the thoughtforms that we have created, not just during this life, but also in all lives. This sounds like an impossible task for one lifetime and it is. Therefore, the process extends over several lifetimes. No one can do it for us. If we are going to become conscious co-creators, we must do it for ourselves. There are great beings who help us with this process when we have the awareness to ask. When asked, Lucifer is able to help us in the Void, while Michael is able to assist us in the manifested world.

There is another way for us to evolve, without doing it ourselves, but it is seldom used. There are highly evolved people who are able to take on the karma of others, eat it and transmute it. This gift is only given occasionally to help people who deeply repent their previous behaviour. It raises the individual to a higher frequency so he or she becomes able to start creating positively in the world. This principle is demonstrated by Jesus when he says to the sinner, "Your sins are forgiven you." He literally was able to transmute another's karma through thought alone. Most of us, however, first need to learn how to do this for ourselves, and then it is very important to teach others how to do it for themselves as well. An effective technique for doing this for others is to pray for them and keep an image in our minds of the best they can be. In this way we help raise their frequency so they can access higher aspects of themselves.

As we work consciously with the mental body, we are working with a subtler, higher frequency. During this process, Lucifer assists us by taking into the Void beliefs and thoughts that we no longer want. Michael assists us to bring into form what we do want. Michael helps us in the conscious world and Lucifer with the subconscious and collective unconscious. We learn to know how to work with both focuses in order to become co-creators.

I would like to share a story that represents how Michael helps us to master the laws of our world and Lucifer helps us to give them up. Both are needed. I remember a time when I was visiting a friend of mine who is a Reiki master. One of her students from Sweden who was also visiting was bending over backward trying to do everything she could to please my friend, including making meals and cleaning the house. My friend, having had enough, said to this woman, "Tanis will cook my dinner." Hurt, the woman left quickly. I asked my friend, "Why don't you want her to help you?" My friend replied, "She's too attached to me. I'm helping her to detach. I've done all my negative karma, now I'm working on giving up my good karma." It is clear to me that the energies of Archangel Michael helped my friend with the first lesson while those of Lucifer, who is great at helping us to give up being "nice", helped her with the second.

Exercise 10: When Do You Grow Most?

Take a moment to still your mind before contemplating your answers to each of these questions and record your observations in your journal.

- ❖ Give three examples of how you have grown in your life during good times.

- ❖ Give three example of how you have you grown when you had to overcome difficulties.

- ❖ Most people would assert that they grew more on an inner level at times of difficulty. Can you name a time when this has been true for you?

In order to grow from the difficulties in our life it is important to see the pearl that is being formed from the grit of sand that is irritating us. This allows us to maintain a sense of humour, faith and perspective in adversity. We also need to realize that the universe gives us only the opportunities that will allow us to grow. It is interested in our success not our failure.

To cleanse the etheric memory body of negative thoughts or feelings that might have resulted from difficult situations, it is helpful to use a visualization of St. Germain, the master who is known as the overseer of the Aquarian Age.

Exercise 11: Visualization to Eliminate Negativity

Take a moment to still your mind before doing the following visualization.

❖ A powerful technique to eliminate old thoughts, feelings and behaviours that you no longer want is to call on St. Germain and say, "Transmute, transmute with the violet fire all that is not of God's desire. I am a being of cause alone; that cause is love, the sacred tone."

❖ As you say these words aloud, or think them in your mind, see a violet fire of purification transmuting all that is not of the light in yourself to the light. The violet colour is purifying in itself as demonstrated by the ultraviolet light that is used in operating rooms to keep everything sterile. It works the same way in this visualization.

It is Lucifer's task to work with laggards, individuals who have fallen into low frequencies. A laggard is someone who is not manifesting his or her highest potential. Any of us can be called a laggard at a certain time in our lives when, through laziness, greed, gluttony, pride or attachments to things of this world, we refuse to learn the lessons presented to us. When we refuse to grow in our entire life, or through a series of lives, then we seriously impede our evolution. If the human race, for example, moves on without us then we will fall to lower frequencies and perhaps be taken to other planets, or solar systems, to continue our evolution there. This has happened to other types of beings who have been laggards in their evolution and who have been brought to Earth to try again. Lucifer works with laggards not just on this planet, but on other planets, and in other solar systems as well. A fuller explanation of laggards is found in the section on Lemuria and Atlantis.

Lucifer can help us with self-love. An appropriate amount of self-love is necessary in order to understand our qualities, gifts and strengths. An excess of self-love leads us to become selfish and egocentric. Think of Lucifer as the one who affects the personality. He teaches the appropriate use of ego and self-will because he is able to come into the lower dimension that most of us consciously or unconsciously inhabit, which we have created by inappropriate use of the ego. It is an evolving process for each of us. When we have setbacks we need to forgive ourselves. Wallowing in self-pity, guilt and self-blame is counterproductive. Instead, we need to recommit to the process of our own spiritual evolution, which is to become a full co-creator.

At this time in our history a division is occurring between people who are embracing the higher frequencies, and those who are clinging to the lower. Even as we observe people who are awakening to consciousness, reading self-help books, talking about chakras and going to acupuncturists, likewise, we see people who are condemning these same things. This is a temporary state of affairs. It may last for hundreds of years and create difficulties based on lack of understanding between the two groups, but the upward path to consciousness truly is the path of evolution. It will not fail and is only a question of time.

As you read this book, the information might be difficult for you to take in. It might fatigue, confuse, or even upset you. Some of these emotions stem from the fact that the information differs from what you have been taught. Much of it calls for people to rise to higher frequencies to access it. Yes, it's written in English, and you understand English. Yet all subjects of discussion strike a certain note in the etheric and other bodies. If we talk about sex, for example, we can imagine which chakras are stimulated. Quite different chakras are stimulated when we discuss esoteric topics. Sometimes we need to stretch ourselves to hear the notes.

Quite simply, what we read, see, and listen to affects our frequency. You might have noticed that sometimes you are feeling joyful and full of life and then you turn on the TV to watch the news. Within a few minutes you are depressed and de-energized. Why? Because almost all news is negative. Reading some of this information might also de-energize you, but for different and positive reasons. In reading *Decoding Your Destiny* some of you are exercising spiritual muscles that most people do not exercise. Doing so might be fatiguing. Now that you have had so much practice, you are ready for the next topic, which might be like running a spiritual marathon.

Evolution of the Els

There are other groups of beings, beside angels, who interact with humanity and have done so for a long time. We know this because cultures around the world have stories and myths about great beings who taught them and who were like gods to them. In more recent times, these myths have been replaced by stories of UFOs, crop circles and physical interactions with beings from other worlds.

Many of these beings are our older brothers and sisters, who are themselves evolving into conscious co-creators, and in the near future humans will join this community. Therefore, it is important to know both our own spiritual history, as well as that of those who have helped us the most. Among these races are the *Els* who, like humans, are co-creators in training. Because they have walked the path to enlightenment ahead of us, they are able to help show us the way.

Els, also known in the Christian and Jewish traditions as the Elohim and Elders, were among the first to leave the Creator. Els, as a type of being, do not exist in the third dimension anymore, but the Akashic Records contain knowledge of their evolution. There are many gradations and states of consciousness for both Els and humans. At present, however, the majority of Els live consciously in the eighth up to tenth dimensions, which are five to seven dimensions above where the majority of humans are conscious.

When the Creator birthed the Els and other beings, he breathed into them as much consciousness as they could hold. Els, unlike angels, were given free will to uncover their essence for themselves and to evolve their specific function. The Creator then made stars as homes for the various beings, and the Els were given Sirius. Separated from the Creator by the lower frequency of the manifested world, the Els knew loneliness for the first time. Yet they were still happy learning new things in these lower dimensions. They asked the Creator for other sentient life forms to share their world and were given them. This was the time of innocence, like the first Garden of Eden before the fall.

The Els have two particular gifts. Within the body of the Creator, the Els are his lungs. Lungs are the container for the Holy Spirit, the breath of life. Performing this function the Els bring the Holy Spirit, the breath of life, to all living beings including humans.

To understand their second function, it is helpful to examine the symbolic meaning behind their name. The letters E and L are very direct, masculine and focused, and these are qualities of the Els. Els have clear sight and the ability to know the truth—one might say intuitively—but this word does not completely encompass their knowing. They also have a clear sense of purpose, direction, dedication and consecration—qualities often applauded in warriors—and, in human terms, there is a warrior sense about them.

Els may appear stern, uncompromising, and even harsh taskmasters in their supreme dedication to achieving the Creator's goals. In this quality they are similar to the angels, who embody one quality and manifest this quality wherever they go. The difference between the two races is that Els act with free will; angels do not. Think, therefore, of the self-restraint and discipline that the Els have learned, since leaving the heart of the Creator, in order not to misuse their free will.

Els, like humans, joined an evolutionary path to consciousness and Els have completed the necessary steps to awaken as conscious co-creators. When we awaken we no longer need to re-enter the evolutionary path that controls space and time in the manifested world. We are free of the cycle of death and rebirth. We are free to choose to continue our evolution in higher dimensions on other planets, or solar systems, or to return to lower dimensions to help other beings. When the Els completed their ascension, (a name given to the ability to leave the physical form to unite with the Divine), many decided to help humans in their evolution.

They help humans in two ways. One group of Els delayed taking their ascension and continue to reincarnate until every human is also ascended. In the Buddhist tradition beings who do this are called bodhisattvas. A second group of Els, who did ascend, help humanity from higher planes of existence.

Els, as a race of beings, have strength on the first ray of will. The quality of will manifests differently in the various states of our development and humans can learn more about the use of will from Els. An unenlightened human is self-centered, and has a strong will to serve him or herself. To awaken we need to commit our ego and self-will to the divine will and to serve others. The Els passed this test long ago and are helping humans in this capacity.

Originally Els lived in the twelfth dimension in the Sirian solar system where they still were in union with the Divine Spirit. When newer beings came to Sirius, the frequency became slower and heavier until whole areas were clouded over, and Els were pulled down to as low as the seventh dimension. At that time some Els chose to rise again to higher dimensions to be in unity with spirit, but many chose to stay in lower dimensions to help the beings there to re-unite with the Divine. This was difficult, because when beings enter lower dimensions in order to create with form, they lose their consciousness of unity with the Divine.

The Creator made new planets, including the Earth, to accommodate the various kinds of beings living in lower dimensions, and many Els volunteered to go to help. These Els had several motivations for doing this. They were ashamed of their increasingly low frequency, and longed to redeem themselves, and also, they wished to help others who were worse off than them. The Els came to Earth as caretakers of others and some of our ancient religious texts refer to this.

Ancient Canaan encompassed Israel, Palestine, Lebanon and Syria and was the birthplace of the ancient Semitic religions. In Canaanite texts, from which both Greek and Hebrew Biblical stories derive, the supreme deity is called El meaning *God*. He is the final authority in all affairs human and divine. One of his titles was *Ab Adam* meaning *Father of Man* and he was the *Creator of all things created*. He was described as an elderly deity who stayed away from daily affairs although he would resolve disputes that the other gods brought to him.

His home was in the area of the Tigris and Euphrates—which later became Sumeria—and he was described as the kindly and merciful one.

To become full co-creators with Spirit, as the Els have done, we must learn to work with all twelve rays of energy. The first ray of creation is the strongest for the Els. It is that of the pioneer who births new ideas and things in the world. El Morya, an Elohim, is the head of the first ray and he oversees the development of wisdom schools on Earth. (See the *Appendix* on page 196 for more information on the rays.)

In order to create a form for the new idea you need great energy, focus and commitment, all of which are qualities of the first ray of divine will. This is why leaders of new ways of thinking, or new types of organisations, have a driven quality. This is true for people like Mother Theresa, Martin Luther King, the Dalai Lama and political leaders such as Gorbachev and Nelson Mandela. Although some people learn to work with the first ray, it may not be their natural strength. The Els can teach them to use this quality.

Just as some humans are hybrids who came originally from angelic evolution, some humans are hybrid Els. Often El-human hybrids have strong will and a pioneering spirit for starting new things and, when spiritually developed, they devote this will to helping others. Unlike angelic-human hybrids, who have a tendency towards emotion, feeling and devotion, El-human hybrids are primarily mental. They are interested in creating forms, organizations, books, modules and systems that work. Others are attracted to them because of their clear, focused thinking. This does not mean that humans from El evolution lack love, any more than humans from angelic evolution lack wisdom. Humans of El descent demonstrate their love primarily through their unswerving commitment to serve the divine will. This is more like the objective love of a priest, rather than the softer, more personal love of humans of angelic descent. Els will sacrifice personal relationships to serve the Divine, which is not always the case of angel-human hybrids. In yogic terms an angelic hybrid might be attracted more to Bhakti (devotional) yoga and an El hybrid more to Jnana (mental) yoga.

Often, we learn the most from a person who is our opposite, rather than one who is similar. For example, Paramahansa Yogananda was primarily on the ray of love. His teacher, Sri Yukteswar, was primarily on the ray of wisdom. Likewise, humans of angelic descent are often attracted to humans of El descent from whom they learn discernment and detachment. The El hybrid learns compassion and gentleness from the angel hybrid. Jesus who taught love is of angelic descent, and Gautama Buddha who taught wisdom is of El descent. These paths of love and wisdom are both needed to become a co-creator and often an individual will change paths for a lifetime, or for many lifetimes, to balance these two qualities.

When the Els first came to Earth in order to help developing life forms, the planet was misty and not yet formed. The Els and other types of beings were the hands of the Creator that created the Earth. This does not mean the Els were perfect. Many of them were attracted to the sensuality of the Earth and fell to even lower frequencies. Because their talent was building form, it makes sense that they were attracted to the material world and experiences of the senses. Humans resemble the Els in both talents and weaknesses. We can learn from the experience of the Els that all of us can fall again, no matter how high we have risen. It is imperative that we do not become arrogant and believe that we are beyond certain temptations.

There were steps in falling and not just one fall. It was a fall for the Els to leave the Creator's heart to go to Sirius where they became heavier. Then it was another fall to come to Earth where they became heavier still. The falls which the Els have had are common to many races of beings including humans.

Falls affect even our day-to-day life, and each of us vibrates at a certain frequency that rises and falls depending on our thoughts and actions. If we eat more vegetables and less meat, meditate and think well of others, our frequency rises. If we gorge on alcohol, sugar and cigarettes, it decreases. If we are depressed and speak badly of others, our energy decreases. It increases when we think well of others and of ourselves.

My diet is changeable and I listen to what my body wants and respond to its needs. I have recently become a vegan although for many years my preferred diet was vegetarian with fish and eggs regularly. This has been a very easy transition as my body has led the change. I am not strict and, as I travel a great deal, I remain flexible to what is available in my environment. I believe that my body prefers not to eat animal products as the frequency of the Earth is moving to higher frequencies of consciousness and I am being called to do so as well. Eating vegetables, grains and fruits assists with this process. Coffee, sweets and wine move in and out of my diet. I love them and sometimes I include them knowing that they bring my energies to lower frequencies. This is not always a bad thing as I am actively living in this world and need to be grounded. At other times they are not in my diet.

Exercise 12: Increasing Your Energy

Take a moment to still your mind before answering the following questions and record your observations in your journal.

❖ When you listen to your body what food does it prefer?

❖ Do you eat the foods your body chooses?

❖ It is obvious that your thoughts and feelings either increase or decrease your energy. What thoughts about yourself or others increase your energy?

❖ What thoughts about yourself or others decrease your energy?

If we witness the effect of our thoughts on our bodies in such a short period of time, just imagine the effect over a lifetime. We have free will to choose on a moment-to -moment basis if we will raise or lower our frequency. With free will we are able to choose to participate consciously in creating according to spiritual laws. Some days and weeks are better than others. Sometimes we are able to change our thoughts and behaviours by ourselves. Other times it is necessary to ask for assistance both from the Creator and from more evolved life forms, and it will be given. This is exactly what the Els did.

When the Els on the Earth had fallen to such a low frequency that they were no longer able to help either themselves or those in their charge, they asked beings from other stars for help. Not all races of beings from other evolutions have the same problems or tests as Earth inhabitants. Every planet has its own unique strengths, weaknesses and tests, and beings that evolve on a planet have these same qualities. Earth is 75 percent water and each of us has exactly the same proportion of water when we are born. This indicates that our greatest test has to do with balancing our emotions, which is the water element. When humans achieve this equilibrium, they radiate the highest emotions of love-compassion known in our galaxy. It is the special gift of the human race.

The Els who entered human evolution became hybrids, no longer the same as the Els who had stayed on Sirius. These El-human hybrids fell to lower frequencies than the Els who remained on Sirius and learned how to work with form in these lower dimensions. These hybrids learned how to use light and energy to manifest what they wanted in the lower frequencies of form. In addition, they also developed a stronger consciousness of self, as well as the quality of love-compassion from being on the Earth.

There were two dangers that the Els who came to Earth discovered. The first was sensuality. The second was self-love. These are the same two dangers that each human must face in his or her journey to consciousness. Through sensuality and the pleasures of our five senses we might develop addictions to the physical world. And through inappropriate self-love, we might exaggerate our uniqueness and separateness, and no longer realise that we are part of the whole of existence.

Sanat Kumara, Buddha, Christ: Wayshowers for Humanity

There are many great beings, as well as Lucifer, Archangel Michael and El Morya who have been involved in humanity's evolution. Sanat Kumara, the Lord of Venus, is one of the greatest. Both Lucifer and Venus are referred to as the Morning Star, and their purposes are linked. Whereas Lucifer helps humanity and other beings discover self-love, Sanat Kumara assists us in learning to love others. Venus has been associated with love in our myths for good reason. When Earth was at its darkest time and unable to hold its light and consciousness, other beings were asked to help. Sanat Kumara, the Lord of Venus, responded and came for many thousands of years to hold Earth from sinking into the Void, into unconsciousness.

Venus is a more evolved planet than Earth and more is said on this topic in the chapter *Life on Planets in our Solar System* on page 171. Sanat Kumara is more highly evolved than any of humanity's evolution. Because he is able to hold Venus in its place in the solar system, he is also able to hold Earth, which is lower in evolution and frequency. Sanat Kumara did this at a time when no humans were evolved enough to do so.

Sanat Kumara was also a teacher and wayshower for Gautama, who became Buddha, and Jesus, who became the Christ. Both Buddha and Christ are titles given to individuals of high levels of consciousness. Gautama the Buddha was the first human to ascend from the Earth through the path of wisdom, as Jesus the Christ was the first through the path of love. These are two aspects of the second ray of love-wisdom. Buddha is now Lord of the Earth, which freed Sanat Kumara to return to Venus in order to assist its inhabitants with their evolution. Buddha and Jesus the Christ, in turn, became guides for evolving humans.

This story exemplifies a spiritual law whereby an individual with greater gifts is responsible for helping others with less developed gifts. This is a law that extends into all walks of life.

Both Buddha and Christ assist Earth and its inhabitants to evolve consciously, but their specific functions are different. Buddha's role as Lord of the Earth is to help the entire Earth and all sentient beings. Included is the planet itself as well as animals, birds, fish, plants and everything that lives on it. Buddha achieves his purpose by anchoring the light given by the Sun onto the Earth. Earth inhabitants are given the right amount of food—in the form of energy that they can assimilate—in order to develop. To accomplish this task, Buddha works with highly developed beings called *Devas* of the plant, mineral and other kingdoms, as well as with humans.

Christ, on the other hand, works specifically with human evolution through a hierarchy of Masters. Christ overshadowed Jesus at his baptism and united with him at that time. Jesus of Nazareth had prepared lifetime after lifetime to be able to hold the energies of Christ who is a cosmic being sent by the Creator, the Great Central

Sun, to Earth. Christ is a Solar Lord and Jesus was the personality vessel that held the energy of Christ. Together they became a soul-infused personality, marking for us the path that each of us must take as our personalities unite with our soul. In an earlier incarnation Christ entered the personality known as Krishna, and it can be seen that the teachings of Krishna in the Bhagavad Gita are very similar to those of Jesus in the New Testament.

Many people believe that Christ will materialize physically on Earth in the near future and are waiting for this to happen. This is not a time to wait to be saved. Instead, it is a time to be proactive in raising our frequencies so that we can access the higher dimensions in which Christ dwells. As each of us takes responsibility for doing this, it draws a stronger cord of energy between the Earth and Christ. This, in turn, allows Christ to access the consciousness of more individuals to increase the speed of their evolution. As this happens, Buddha simultaneously is helping Earth to raise her consciousness by bringing her more light and energy. Buddha and Christ, working together, are greatly affecting the rise in consciousness of all beings on this planet.

Christ is a lord of compassion who, as the shepherd we hear of in the Bible, leaves all the sheep that are safe and goes out to seek the one who is lost. Unconscious humans are these lost sheep. Christ is also a lord of justice who stands at the door of each individual's heart. The key to open this door to consciousness is love, wisdom and commitment to serve divine will. This opening occurs in the third, fourth and fifth levels of spiritual transformation that he oversees. These stages are exemplified by three major tests that Jesus undertook for us to witness. Jesus achieved the third level in the garden of Gethsemane when he committed to do the divine will over his own will. The fourth level occurred when he forgave those who crucified him. The fifth level was when he ascended and was able to manifest a body that could move through space and time.

When we master the third level of consciousness, we are able to access information that would have been dangerous to others and ourselves before that time. For example, we are able to see the soul's purpose of other people and assist them to raise their consciousness. Also, we are able to work with sentient life forms on other planets and solar systems. These life forms have been protected from us, and us from them, until our frequency was high enough to make conscious contact.

It is important to remember that the same spiritual principles exist on each level of existence and consciousness. For example, the law of twelve to one is a universal principle in evolution. Christ's disciple, the Master Jesus, had twelve disciples for this specific reason. Each disciple had a specific gift and each of these strengths was on a different ray of energy that flows from the Sun to us. Peter, for example, was on the first ray of will and power. That is why he was the perfect choice to build the organization of the Christian church, which needed the pioneering energy and determined focus that Peter had.

In lower dimensions a spiritual teacher who is still in a physical body takes responsibility for twelve others, who are slightly behind him or her on the evolutionary spiral. These twelve could be students and might also be children, parents, friends and co-workers who do not know consciously that they are with their teacher. Although the teacher may be more spiritually evolved than the twelve, the twelve might have superior gifts that they teach or share with the teacher. The spiritual teacher could be learning qualities such as tolerance, forgiveness and humility or could be benefiting from the practical skills of the twelve others.

A grid of light which links all individuals at all levels works in multiples of twelve up to our Sun, and even past the Sun to the Creator. At each stage, we progress to higher levels of responsibility for serving others and the divine will on this planet.

The Principle of Twelve to One

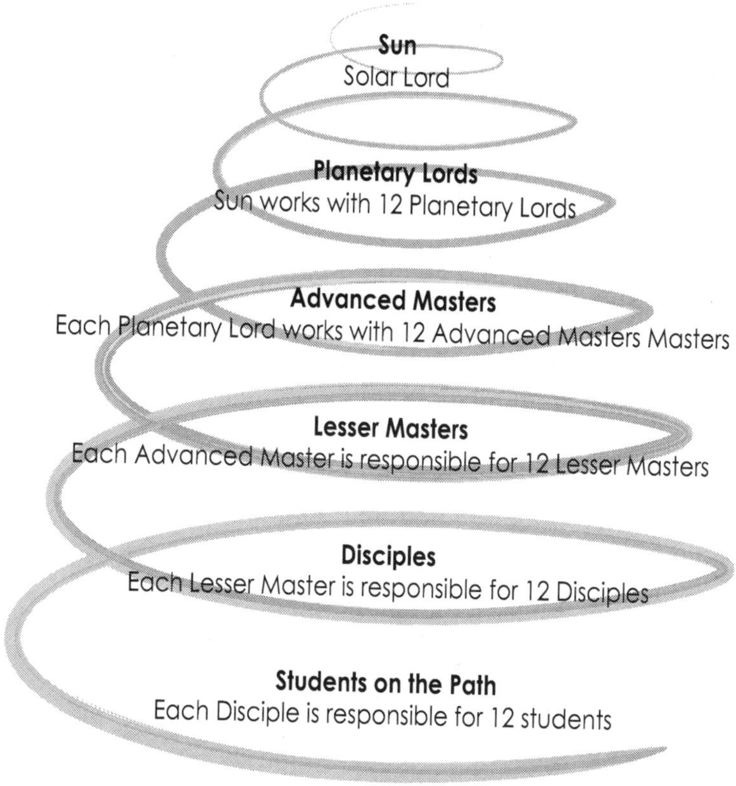

Sun
Solar Lord

Planetary Lords
Sun works with 12 Planetary Lords

Advanced Masters
Each Planetary Lord works with 12 Advanced Masters Masters

Lesser Masters
Each Advanced Master is responsible for 12 Lesser Masters

Disciples
Each Lesser Master is responsible for 12 Disciples

Students on the Path
Each Disciple is responsible for 12 students

Figure 6 - A visual guide to assess your relationship within the spiritual hierarchy of this Solar System.

There are two main spiritual affiliations to which I belong. In one I am a student of El Morya who oversees the creation of all esoteric groups on Earth. Some of these esoteric traditions include that of Paramahansa Yogananda, Rudolph Steiner and the Dalai Lama among others and my work helps to form bridges between their teachings and to bring this into our current time.

In the second spiritual group I am responsible for helping others develop their spiritual consciousness. This group consists of students with our International Institute for Transformation as well as some of my family and friends who are not studying formally with me. In addition to my work during the day, I work with members of my official and unofficial groups during my sleep state as well as working with others who are not embodied at this time. It is important to mention that not everyone in my spiritual group knows that I am their teacher and it is not necessary for me to state this. This is something they discover in their own journey even as I continue to discover the other members of my personal spiritual group.

Exercise 13: Your Spiritual Group of Twelve

Take a moment to still your mind before answering the following questions. Record your observations in your journal.

- ❖ Begin to identify the spiritual group of twelve to which you belong. These individuals may be friends, relatives, colleagues or people you know only slightly.

- ❖ Have you ever had a spiritual teacher? Do you have one now? What is the main talent and focus of this teacher? Does your teacher also have a teacher, either incarnated or not incarnated? If so, what is that teacher's focus?

- ❖ If you have difficulty answering the previous questions, are you inspired by a specific spiritual or influential figure such as Mother Theresa, the poet Rumi, Deepak Chopra or Pema Chodrin? These individuals may be wayshowers to indicate where to look for your spiritual group of twelve.

Section Three

CYCLES OF HUMAN EVOLUTION

Playing with Matter

No rules hold me.
I rise, fall, build and tear down.
I hold, release, yearn and hold again.
Gently, firmly, it's all the same.
Playing with matter, that's the game.

Creating Form: The First Cycle

Humans have engaged in a very lengthy period of evolution to develop their physical, emotional, mental and spiritual bodies. This period can be divided into seven main cycles from our incarnation on the misty Earth in the far distant past, to our present state as a technological culture, and to our near future as enlightened beings.

The human body was in seed form in the first cycle of our evolution. It had only rudimentary centers that would allow it to become a fully developed human. These energy systems called chakras were also in seed form. They receive information and energy from Spirit. Each of us has twelve chakras, located in our etheric body, which allow us to work with Solar and Earth energy to feed our physical, emotional, mental and higher bodies. The five chakras working in the unmanifested world will not be addressed. We are concerned at this time with the seven chakras that work in the manifested world. They are as follows:

- The root chakra is located at the base of the spine. It connects us to the Earth.

- The second chakra, the sacral centre, facilitates our sexual and emotional expressions.

- The third chakra, the solar plexus, controls our will.

- The fourth, our heart chakra, allows us to love and have compassion.

- The throat, our fifth chakra, is associated with communication and creativity.

- The sixth, the brow chakra or third eye, relates to intuition.

- The seventh, or crown chakra, located above our physical head, connects to the Divine.

Originally, these chakras were designed to enable humans to fulfill the function of drawing energy from the Sun to give to the Earth. However, in our present state most humans draw more energy for themselves than they give. This will change as we rise into higher levels of consciousness to become energy donors to the Earth and its inhabitants. Els, and other beings who assisted in our creation, worked with these chakras to build our bodies. They began in the first cycle of humanity's evolution to activate the root chakra, so it would anchor humans to the planet, helping to create a denser form.

When conscious beings, such as the Els from Sirius and the Pleiadians, first came to Earth, the planet was like mist. It was neither solid nor liquid, but between water and gas. That is how Earth appeared when humanity began on this planet. However, it was not humanity as we know it now. When scientists speak about the pool of various chemicals and compounds which came together to birth the Earth, that is an appropriate image. Sirians and Pleiadians came to assist with the creation of consciousness on this planet. By projecting their thoughts and etheric bodies, they created a denser, more substantial form out of the existing gas.

The five bodies that compose the human personality vessel that houses the soul were present on Earth in seed form during this time. Let's take a moment to explore the five bodies that comprise the personality vessel. This information is essential to an understanding of the spiritual laws that are being discussed in this book. We are physical, etheric, emotional, mental and soul beings, and we need to develop all five bodies in equal strength in order to become full co-creators with spirit. These bodies interpenetrate each other and are differentiated by frequency.

- The physical body is what most people think of as their only body. It is the densest of the four, has the lowest frequency and can be seen in the third dimensional world. Too much emphasis on the physical and we are inflexible, stubborn, and attached to what we think is true. We are unable to accept new ideas, which can lead to not rising in consciousness.

- The etheric body, sometimes called the subtle physical, is the blueprint or memory body. It determines what we look like physically, our temperament and mental gifts. Our etheric body is built each lifetime, and is based on which parts of our soul and past lives we wish to work on in this life. By learning to work with our etheric body we can cure illness, erase negative thoughts and reprogram ourselves in positive ways.

- The emotional body is where our feelings are housed. Our preferences, likes and dislikes, fears and passions are all recorded there. With too much emotion we might cry too much, become despondent, and not be able to listen to positive suggestions from others.

- The mental body is what we associate with our rational thought and decision making. It is the "me", our personal identity and name. With too much emphasis on the lower mental we overvalue logic, facts and information, and undervalue feelings.

- The astral body is non-local and, can simultaneously be both in the physical body and anywhere else in the universe. This is our dream body, with which we travel and see outside time and space.

- The higher mental body is where thought creates reality. Too much strength in the higher mental body can lead to self-righteousness, elitism, psychic instability and detachment from the Earth and the human experience. It can lead to the inability to have relationships with others and all living things, or to function in the world.

- The soul, or causal body, is where spirit condenses into form as an individual soul.

Each time we are born we relearn how to use each of the five bodies and their associated chakras, corresponding to a certain cycle in human evolution. For example, a child first masters the physical world by learning to walk. Next, she learns to control her emotions. Following this, the child learns to think logically. Finally, she develops inner knowing. At any of these stages difficulties and wounds can occur. If we examine the cycles that we have gone through in human evolution, we are able to better understand what to do to repair these bodies.

The Els, Pleiadians and others, who were helping to create the Earth, worked in higher dimensions and did not have a solid form in the first cycle of human evolution. Any form they had was more ghost-like, which is what humans looked like as well in the first cycle of human evolution. Our guardians and nurturers weren't yet working in the physical realm, but more in the etheric. They were given the blueprint of Earth and its inhabitants, and they built according to this blueprint. In the future, humans will learn how to do this for other races of beings once we have learned to fully work with our higher bodies.

This creation period went on for a very long time, but time had no meaning for them, as they were immortal and lived above the fourth dimension of time and space. Such thoughts would never have occurred to the Els or Pleiadians, because they were creating at the still point in the turning world. That is the place where space balances between the manifested and the unmanifested world. In that place, there is no time. When these beings were able to create more density, even though it was still misty and not Earth as we know it today, then the second cycle in evolution commenced.

In the first cycle of Earth evolution, prototype or primitive humans mastered the etheric body, creating form and planting the seeds that would develop in further cycles.

Seven Cycles of Humanity's Evolution*

Cycle	Name	Chakra	Body	Function
1	Creating Form	Root	Etheric	Plant seeds to ripen in later cycles
2	Hyperborean	Root/ Sacral	Physical	Create a dense physical body
3	Lemurian	Sacral/ Third Eye	Emotional	Evolution into 2 paths: individuation vs. group soul
4	Atlantean	Solar Plexus	Lower Mental	Create through Will
5	Colonies	Heart	Astral	Science, mathematics and human law aligned to Divine Law. Learn to help others
6	Historical Age	Solar Plexus/ Throat	Lower Mental/ Etheric template	Intellectual and technological achievements
7	Enlightened Human	Crown	Higher Mental/Causal	Conscious co-creation with Divine Laws

Figure 7 - A summary chart of the human cycles from the divine creation of form throughout time to humans as co-creators.

*In this chart the dominant chakra(s) being activated are mentioned although other chakras are also functioning especially in the higher cycles of evolution.

Hyperborea: The Second Cycle

The ancient Celts referred to beings of the second cycle of human evolution as the Hyperboreans. These are the same ones whom the Egyptians spoke of as the inhabitants of the land of Punt, which was their mythical Eden that was supposedly located south of Egypt in Africa. In ancient Greek myth the second cycle was the time of the Titans, the Cyclops and other mythical beings with whom the Greek Gods fought. The Greek Gods were the Atlanteans and their battles with the Titans reveal what happens when one age replaces another; in that case when the third cycle replaced the second cycle.

Mentally and emotionally Hyperboreans were more like animals. They lacked individuality. They were, however, able to work with elements of earth and the lower two chakras in order to manifest bodies of various shapes and sizes. They experimented with building form based on a specific quality. The primitive statues and drawings of the Earth Mother, which are found in native cultures around the world, show her with exaggerated hips, stomach, and thighs, representing the storage of power that the Hyperboreans held in their lower body.

Whereas in the first cycle of Earth evolution, primitive humans mastered the etheric body, in the second cycle the Hyperboreans mastered the physical. Perhaps "mastered" is too strong a word as we continue to master these bodies until we awaken. However, Hyperboreans achieved a working knowledge and comfort with these two bodies.

And what has become of these Hyperboreans? During that ancient time, the Sun increased the energy it sent to Earth, and the mist began to be burnt off. The Hyperboreans could no longer live on the outside of the Earth when the mist started to disappear so they moved inside the Earth. Their evolved descendants now live in the inner heart of the Earth and work with the evolution of the Earth's consciousness. You can read more about them in their specific chapter *Beings of the Inner Earth* on page 125.

At that time, our planet did not have as much dry land as it does today. There was one large land mass called Gondwanaland. The second cycle ended with a pole shift during which time Gondwanaland broke into many pieces that we refer to as continents. The humans continued their evolution on an island in the Pacific Ocean called Lemuria. Even today remnants of Lemuria are found in the series of islands from Hawaii to Easter Island. All have identical flora and fauna revealing their common ancestor.

In the second cycle, Hyperboreans worked with root and sacral chakras, creating a dense physical body.

Lemuria: The Third Cycle

The third cycle of Earth evolution during which we began to take on a more recognizably human form, was in Lemuria, also known as Mu. The words "mare" and "mer" descend from Lemuria and both words, one Latin and one French, mean sea. In English, the word sea has two meanings. Sea is a large body of water and "to see" means to perceive clearly, and these two meanings are linked in the Lemurian cycle. In the third cycle humans learned to see clearly physically and to master the emotional body, which is linked to the water element.

The brow chakra, or third eye, is linked to the sacral chakra, which is the emotional centre, and Lemurians were developing clarity in emotions. This means that they were developing preferences for what they liked and didn't like in terms of relationships with others and their environment. With the development of the emotional body, humans began to individualize and form unique and complex personalities.

Lemurians were very attracted to water and they loved to swim. Some of them spent more time in the water than on land and started to adapt to water existence. Our myths of mermaids come from this cycle of evolution. Dolphins are part of the human race who broke away in Lemuria and decided to continue their evolution in the water. Dolphins, conscious of their early connection to humanity, have been known to rescue drowning people and bring them to land. Many cultures, including the ancient Greeks, recognized that dolphins were once human. There is much physical evidence attesting to our common ancestry. All the bones found in human hands and arms exist in dolphin flippers. Scientists are moving in the direction that will allow them in the not so distant future, to discover the genetic link between dolphins, whales and that other mammal—humans.

Just as Angels and Els have entered human evolution and are now hybrids, so some dolphins have re-entered human evolution. They teach humans play, harmony, healing, sensuality, sexuality and love. Attesting to their gifts in these and other areas, dolphins in captivity work with autistic children and cancer patients.

The evolution of whales differs somewhat from that of dolphins. Although both dolphins and humans chose the path of becoming individuals in Lemuria, whales chose to continue their evolution as a group soul. Whales are immense partly because they are housing not one but many individuals. Whale and dolphin intelligence are not the same, because when a being decides not to develop an individual ego its learning and personal growth are directed differently. This happened in Lemuria when these group souls didn't enter individualization, which was to be their next step in development.

Whales have now evolved as a group soul. They swim in pods and often, when one beaches itself to end its life, the group will all beach themselves to end their lives. This illustrates the power of the group soul, when a being does not develop individual consciousness or make decisions for itself. It is important to note that in other solar systems sentient life forms are able to evolve as group souls, so this is not a lesser form of consciousness but a different one. Whales, in fact, work with the collective unconscious of humanity and these deep sea divers are now bringing this collective unconscious back to the surface for humanity to reintegrate into its consciousness. Much of our collective memory of our ancient past will resurface as this happens.

During the Lemurian cycle approximately 400,000 years ago, beings from another solar system created a colony on Earth. They were more highly advanced than the primitive humans living on Earth at that time. The creation myths of the Sumerians predate those of the Old Testament of the Bible and are very detailed in their description of these gods that created them. According to these accounts the Annuna (called Anunnaki by the Babylonians) were sent to Earth due to their unacceptable behaviour on their own planet. These Laggards came in primitive spacecraft, not unlike where we are at today, and their penance likely involved mining gold in Africa, which archaeological evidence has shown is the location from which the earliest humans have come.

According to the Sumerians, Anu was the head god who resided mostly on his home planet of Nibiru and only occasionally checked on what was happening on Earth. His two sons, Enlil and Enki, oversaw the mining on Earth.

W. G. Lambert and A. R. Millard who wrote *Atra-Hasis: the Babylonian Story of the Flood* pieced together fragments both of Babylonian and Assyrian accounts, based on earlier Sumerian texts, which described the mutiny of the Anunnaki. The Anunnaki rebelled against their overseers and this mutiny occurred approximately 300,000 to 200,000 years ago. It was at this time that they interfered with human evolution.

These ancient accounts tally with current archaeological evidence, which puts the birthplace of modern humanity in the same area of Africa as the Babylonian accounts. In 2003, *Scientific American, Special Edition, New Look at Human Evolution,* it is stated that fossils found in Chad, Kenya and Ethiopia now extend the human record back to 7 million years. In the same edition we find that "Archaeologists believe that hominids of modern body form most likely emerged in Africa around 150,000 years ago and co-existed with other hominids for a time before emerging as the only species leading to modern man."

According to the ancient Babylonian record, the Anunnaki mixed the DNA of primitive humans with their own genetic material. The Els, who had brought the Earth to its state of evolution, were horrified as this was against karmic law. According to Berossus, writing the history of Babylon in the 3rd century BCE, the deity Marduk (equated to Enki and also called Bel meaning *Lord*) brought forth hideous beings. Some men had legs and horns of goats. Some men had human heads and torsos with horse hindquarters. Bulls were also bred with men's heads. We recognize these descriptions as the Satyr-faun, Centaur and Minotaur of the Greek myths. Some of these were the failed first attempts at genetic engineering in which the Anunnaki were involved. Others were prototypes of other evolving species that the Anunnaki were mimicking.

According to Babylonian texts, the head god Marduk says:

Blood to blood I join.
Blood to bone I form.
An original thing, its name is man,
Aboriginal man is mine in making.

All his occupations are faithful service,
The gods that fell have rest.

(N. K. Sanders,
Poems of Heaven and Hell from Ancient Mesopotamia)

In other words, humans were created by these Anunnaki to be their slaves. This specialized labor force occurred at a time before there was grain cultivation, fruit planting or cattle raising. Enlil was the chief god living in Sumeria and his brother Enki (whose name means the dragon or snake) headed the group of miners in Africa. The Anunnaki genetically altered native humans, who were developing on Earth, and their chief function was to be miners. Some of these slaves were taken to Sumeria where the governing Anunnaki were living. For the primitive humans, this was like living in Eden.

Originally, these genetically altered humans were sterile and not very intelligent, but Enki (the snake) told them the secrets of how to procreate and give birth. The sharing of this knowledge was not acceptable to Enlil, who wanted only sterile slaves for the mines. A fight ensued during which Enki (Marduk) won. Having been given this knowledge by Enki, the humans were banished from the garden of Eden. The Anunnaki monitored the progress of the developing humans, which is why the book of Genesis in the Bible has a completely accurate record of whom begat whom.

At the same time, the Els were overseeing the development of the primitive humans in Lemuria. The laggard Anunnaki and developing humans were to have been kept separate, but it was inevitable that the Anunnaki, through boredom and seeking a way to ease their work, would seek to influence the developing humans. The primitive humans of Lemuria were more like the great ape of today. These are the missing links that archaeologists seek, and explains why there was a quantum jump in our evolution from Neanderthal to Homo Sapiens some 300,000 years ago.

The Anunnaki influenced the humans, not just through genetic engineering, but also through mental imprinting. The minds of the Laggards were stronger and more developed than those of the Earth races. Bodies had not assumed a fixed shape in Lemuria and still could be altered through thought. If left alone, many would have developed into humanity, which was the original plan, but the Laggards asked them to assume shapes and functions that were not natural to them. In this way animals were created.

Even today the Laggards are influencing humanity. They interbred with humans, much as the Angels and Els did, and their qualities have been passed on to their progeny. One of their main gifts is technological brilliance, which they bring to computers and scientific inventions. Many are still engaged in genetic engineering and the misuse of natural resources. A second gift is strategy and influencing others, which they bring to manipulating others for their own gain in large corporations, and in financial and economic structures.

Not all Laggards harmed the human and animal race. When some came, they chose to start anew. In doing so, they have struggled against their lower imperfect natures for many thousands of years to rise and to help humanity to rise as well. The Laggards initially delayed human evolution, but in the long run, they have been of assistance. They have strengthened our free will and resistance to something that is not pure or true. Also, they have strengthened our persistence, ego and power as we had so much to overcome once the Laggards arrived.

The path of evolution split into many tracks in the Lemurian cycle when dolphins, whales and animals chose different evolutionary paths from humans. Whales and animals chose the path of being a group soul, which is the path of interdependence. Humans who stayed on the land chose the path of becoming distinct individuals with the chief quality of independence. Both qualities are necessary in order for us to become full co-creators. If we overdevelop dependence on the group, we do not learn free will. Conversely, if we cling to our independence at the expense of the group, we become like Laggards.

This third cycle ended with the development of the emotional body in humanity and what we think of as feminine, soft, caring qualities. Except for some islands in the South Pacific, Lemuria sank. When this occurred some Lemurians immigrated to Lake Titicaca in Bolivia and other locations in Central and South America, while others continued their evolution in Atlantis, which was located in the Atlantic Ocean between the United States and the Straits of Gibraltar.

The third cycle of evolution, the Lemurian, opened the third eye and evolved the emotional body. In this cycle, two paths emerged: that of developing as an individual and that of developing as a group soul.

Some individuals are more dependent on others' opinions of them and prefer to follow than to lead. Others are more independent, prefer to lead, and they freely express their opinions. I belong to the latter group and have been an independent thinker from an early age. Much of this stems from the fact that, as a mystic, I literally see and hear what many people do not and have not had others to guide me in developing these qualities.

However, I love to be a follower in areas where others have more expertise. I belong to a hiking group and happily trek after others and am relieved when others lead. This happens in gardening as well because I am fortunate to have master gardeners as friends and they patiently teach me all they know of plants.

I love co-creation and believe that when we put two people together we either have more than two or less than two. I am grateful for the many people in my life who practice co-creation with me where we become more than two. For example, when faced with a problem asking for a solution I am not as attracted to my own answer as I am to the right answer to the problem. I also happily implement others' ideas as freely as I would my own. In this way I practice true co-creation.

Exercise 14:
Dependence, Independence and Interdependence

Take a moment to still your mind before answering the following questions. Optimally, set aside time for three days to contemplate and journal your answers to these questions.

❖ Day One: Which qualities are desirable that build togetherness? Which ones do you have? Which qualities do you wish to develop? How will you develop them?

❖ Day Two: Which qualities do you consider desirable for independence? Which ones do you have? Which ones do you wish to develop? What is your plan to develop them?

❖ Day Three: After we learn dependence and independence we need to learn interdependence. Which qualities of interdependence do you have? Which qualities do you wish to develop? What is your plan to do this?

Atlantis: The Fourth Cycle

For the sake of clarity, Earth evolution is being discussed as various cycles, but it is important to note that in actuality all cycles overlap. In each cycle of evolution a certain quality is developed, which humans need to become a co-creator. The Laggards slowed down this process and as a result, there are individuals from the Lemurian, Atlantean, and later cycles physically on Earth who have not learned the lessons of their cycle. In each cycle of evolution, new beings incarnate for the first time on this planet. This occurs because the Earth has reached a state in its evolution where it can host humans of higher consciousness. The new ones bring in the accumulated wisdom and qualities that humanity has achieved to date. They receive these from the collective unconscious—the Akashic Records for all humans.

To understand how several cycles of humans are able to evolve simultaneously, consider the evolution of the plants on the Earth. Lichen was one of the first plant forms. Then moss entered, followed by grasses, which then became a bush, a tree, and finally a forest. Within this forest, all previous species of plant life might still live, and some might die out to be replaced by more highly evolved species. The older the forest the more diversity that exists. Like plants, humans are at different stages of their evolution. Older races of beings create the soil that allows younger races of beings to survive. Each of us has the responsibility to do the best we can with the raw material we incarnated with and to apply ourselves to fulfilling our purpose.

In the fourth cycle of evolution, called the Atlantean, humans were to develop the lower mental body and bring their will under control so that they could create what they wanted. Added to this, Atlanteans needed to control the etheric, physical and emotional bodies that they had inherited from proceeding evolutions.

The Atlantean evolution was divided into three sub-cycles and it started off with much promise. In the first sub-cycle, Atlantean bodies were a combination of gas, liquid and solid, but not as solid as our bodies today. By that time, the main branches of evolution into animals, dolphins and humanity had been determined and the mind of almost all Atlanteans was very open, receptive and blank. In this first sub-cycle of Atlantis, the Laggards began to negatively imprint the blank mind of humans. Simultaneously, the Atlantean mind was positively imprinted by the environmental beauty, buildings and forms that they had started to build. These buildings were very rudimentary and not yet solid, but they were humanity's first constructions.

In the second sub-cycle of Atlantean evolution, forms were more or less solid. Angels, Els and other guardians still walked and talked with humans at that time. Atlanteans were easily able to see these guardians, as they were more clairvoyant than we are today. They saw the astral, mental, soul/causal and even higher bodies of the guardians, and it was the causal and higher bodies of these guardians that taught and imprinted the Atlantean mind for the good. Atlanteans asked the guardians for advice and then followed it. These guardians were like older brothers and sisters to them. This was not the same as our current time when we view gods as something very different from us. This separation is due to our lack of self-worth and self-acceptance. Atlanteans did not feel this separation because they were still in a period of innocence and had not yet fallen.

Unfortunately, it was during this second sub-cycle that conflict arose between the teachings of the guardians and that of the Laggards. Atlanteans with weaker minds were increasingly imprinted by the lower frequencies of untruth or mixed truth as taught by the Laggards. Those with stronger minds were imprinted by the higher frequencies of truth and love as taught by the guardians. The Laggards appealed to the sensual, animal nature in people. In fact, they still do this today. In Lemuria the Laggards were able to magnify one quality in our animal state, as all of us have one dominant quality in seed form. These seeds blossomed into role differentiation. Some Atlanteans, for example, chose to be builders, while others became priests, healers or gardeners. Atlanteans chose to develop their unique gifts so that they could focus their mental, emotional and physical energy into one area rather than diffusing it. This choosing coincided with the specific talent of each person's individual ray and helped people along the path to development of distinct personalities.

In the third sub-cycle, the bodies of Atlanteans were outwardly much like human bodies are today. Those who vibrated on a higher frequency of love, truth and purity were still in communication with the spiritual guardians. Unfortunately, those vibrating on a lower frequency of deception and untruth were no longer able to see these teachers. Progressively they were cut off from the light and love of the guardians and began to lose their belief that these guardians existed. The falling ones remembered that they had once been able to communicate with guardians and were jealous that others still could. This is where envy first came into our evolution.

This time in our prehistory was no more negative than our present day, and there was much positive. The third sub-cycle of Atlantis was a golden age of science and technology. The knowledge and use of crystal far surpassed our current understanding, with crystals being used in libraries for storing information and knowledge. They also were employed in transportation to energize various kinds of transportation vehicles, and served in devices to receive and transmit communications. Atlanteans at that time understood the laws of gravity and anti-gravity, and had mastered the ability to construct vehicles that would fly. Those people who were evolved in the qualities of purity, truth and love were able to levitate and the skill of telepathy was more developed than it is today.

Three Cycles of Human Evolution in Atlantis

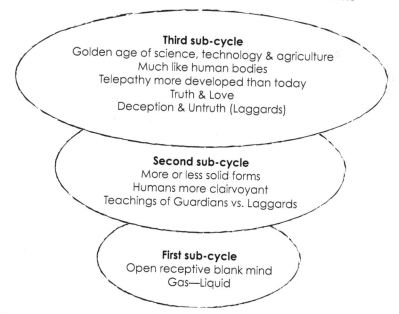

Third sub-cycle
Golden age of science, technology & agriculture
Much like human bodies
Telepathy more developed than today
Truth & Love
Deception & Untruth (Laggards)

Second sub-cycle
More or less solid forms
Humans more clairvoyant
Teachings of Guardians vs. Laggards

First sub-cycle
Open receptive blank mind
Gas—Liquid

Figure 8 - The earlier civilization of Atlantis created a foundation for our modern age.

Cities were more the size of small towns and villages, resembling the ancient city of Knossos on Crete. In centers of healing Atlanteans diagnosed illness using both crystals and highly developed intuition. They healed with herbs, colour, sound, aroma and light. They used surgery only as a last resort, to operate on broken bones or to remove growths in the body. It might sound as if Atlanteans were more advanced than us. However, it's important to remember that Earth's frequency was faster and the atmosphere lighter. Therefore, it was easier to manifest what you wanted than it is now. Even today, there are humans who are able to levitate and demonstrate many of the qualities practiced in Atlantis. In the future we will be able to achieve these and other Atlantean skills through accessing the Akashic Records, where this information is stored.

Atlanteans made great advances in agriculture. They travelled around the planet in their flying and sailing vehicles gathering the fruit, vegetables and grains they domesticated and grew. Highly evolved Atlanteans ate no meat, but the lower ones did. Modern historians know that Neolithic cultures, which grew grain and domesticated animals, existed from 11,000 BCE in the Near East. Yet, history does not know when these significant achievements began. Atlantis is the answer. Since then, no new animals have been domesticated and few new wild grains cultivated.

Some Laggards experimented with existing beings to create new species, which is how the pig came into existence. Pigs were hybrids created by genetic manipulation from combining an animal with a lower human, similar to a Neanderthal. We know medically that pig blood, skin and heart are more similar to those of humans than those of any other animal. Although humans have forgotten this knowledge surrounding the pig's origins, this is the original reason for many religions banning the consumption of pork.

This genetic tampering was not in keeping with the divine plan and was a great error. It is a very dangerous practice, yet scientists currently are experimenting again in these areas. Even now we are raising super pigs for organ donations. Until we can create bodies based on divine law, we are unable to understand the ramifications of genetic engineering, and should abstain from doing it. Many people who are fascinated by crystals, genetic engineering, telepathic communication, and the like are former Atlanteans. They now have the opportunity to review what they learned in their previous incarnation and take this knowledge to a higher frequency.

In the third sub-cycle, called the Golden Age of Atlantis, priests, seers and kings were enlightened. Their hearts grieved for their brothers and sisters who had fallen out of the light and they strove to help them return to consciousness. Nonetheless, the gap between the two grew. Wise Atlanteans saw that Atlantis would come to a bitter and violent end and prepared to leave with the best of their technology, arts and people. Atlantis sank because the Laggards misused the powers of the technologies of that time, such as crystal and anti-gravitational devices, employing them in destructive, egocentric ways. We have come to the same place in our history currently, only several spirals higher, where the Atlanteans made these errors. Our test today is to not repeat these mistakes but to use our technologies for life in keeping with divine law.

Atlantis was destroyed over a period from 24,000 BCE to approximately 10,000 BCE. The later date was when the great flood occurred, which was a tidal wave created by the final sinking of the continent. This story is found in the myths of almost all cultures, as it was a tragedy for us all. Still, it was a cleansing so that the next cycle could commence.

Spiritually evolved Atlanteans travelled to other places on Earth to help developed humans. Some Laggards went with them and cunningly pretended to have repented the error of their ways. Wise Atlanteans never gave up hope that the Laggards would change for the better, but unfortunately, the Laggards who did not do so contaminated everyone they met. Some Laggards, however, did return to the light, which caused great rejoicing in higher dimensions reminiscent of the joy experienced by our Creator when Lucifer was redeemed.

By the time that Atlantis sank some humans had evolved to the point that they could live in the fifth dimension. Some of these went to other planets and solar systems to continue their evolution. Others formed the hierarchy of Ascended Masters to assist their younger brothers and sisters who were still evolving within the cycles of Earth incarnations. This was the first time that it was possible for humans to work as co-creators with the teachers and guardians who had helped them. Although these Ascended Masters still needed guidance and support from the Els and others, they were given the function of assisting their fellow humans to rise to consciousness. During the last 12,000 years—which is very little historical time—the Ascended Masters have grown exponentially in numbers and strength as more humans have ascended to join them. They fulfil their task under the direction of the Christ. Their success has allowed some Els and members of other races to move on to other duties, although some are still on the Earth as hybrid-humans. Some guardians still work with the hierarchy to teach the ascended humans as much of the overall divine plan as they are able to comprehend.

Meanwhile back on Earth, the lower mental body developed in many Atlanteans, but not all of this was positive. The higher mental body, which allows us to consciously create according to divine law, developed only in a few. We must not despair because of this story, for it is all part of the divine plan. As with Lucifer, those who fall the furthest often have the greatest strength when they return to the Creator, and we must see all beings in their perfect state.

Through the fourth cycle of evolution the Atlanteans developed the solar plexus chakra, activating the ability to create through will, and also to work with the lower mental body.

Founding Colonies: The Fifth Cycle

The fifth cycle of human evolution was from approximately 20,000 BCE to 4000 BCE. The former date is collaborated by Egyptian records that set Egypt's founding between 30,000 BCE and 23,000 BCE. The discrepancy depends on whether the Egyptian records are speaking of the earlier or later contacts by the Neters, the eight sons and daughters of the sun god Ra. Ancient Egyptian sources describe a long period during which Egypt was ruled by these Neters who were Els from Sirius who came from Atlantis as guardians and teachers. The most well know of these Neter gods were Osiris, Isis and Horus.

Then in another, almost equally long period Egypt was ruled by the Companions of Horus. These Companions of Horus were Atlanteans who had been taught by Osiris, Isis and Horus, and they established colonies among others in Egypt, Sumeria, British Isles, Indus Valley of India, Tibet and New Zealand. In South and North America these colonies included the Mayan, Cherokee, Haida and Hopi cultures. When Atlantis was destroyed around 10,000 BCE, centres of light established by Atlanteans already existed in these colonies.

Is there any archaeological evidence of these Atlantean colonies? In his book, *Underworld, The Mysterious Origins of Civilization*, Graham Hancock asserts that in the antediluvian world Sri Lanka was attached to southern India, and Malta to Sicily via a 60 kilometre land bridge. In January of 2002 Indian marine scientists discovered extensive remains in the Gulf of Cambay, a site that spans an area of 25 square kilometres, 35 metres deep. About 2,000 man-made artefacts have been dredged and carbon-dated from 8,500 to 9,500 years old. Likewise, Malta has very old ruins, whose builders remain unknown. Underwater structures off the coast of Japan at Yonaguni reveal megaliths, stone circles, ramps and other formations. When scientists are able to change their paradigm to include the possibility of Atlantis, they will see proof in these and other stone remains.

Strong genetic evidence indicates that the earliest Americans did not find their way from Siberia by way of a land bridge, as was previously thought. The Ojibwa around the Great Lakes, for example, have an unusual mitochondrial DNA, not found in Asia at all but in Europe over 15,000 years ago. Also, a early stone-age flint tool called the Clovis point, used by the ancestors of the Lascaux Caves in France 30,000 years ago, has been found in North America. For this to happen, communication between Europe and North America had to have been possible.

At the beginning of the fifth cycle, there was a great gap in consciousness between the Atlanteans and the native humans who lived on the rest of the planet. The native humans were evolving through the more animal-like evolution described in the earlier cycles. The Atlanteans, on the other hand, were seeded on Earth by races from other solar systems and so had a head start in consciousness. Are humans descended from an ape-like ancestor, who evolved from one-celled organisms in the chemical sea of Earth billions of years ago, or are humans descended from star beings? Both answers are valid.

Neanderthals and other early hominids developed from animal humans who had been genetically engineered by the Laggards in Africa some 300,000 years ago. What we call Modern Man, or Homo Erectus, came from Atlantean evolution. Neanderthals and Homo Erectus interbred. Humanity's myths describe this as the Gods (Zeus, for example) breeding with humans. Archaeological evidence supports the fact of interbreeding as well as seen in *Scientific American, Special Edition,* referred to earlier. Archaeologists state that Modern Man emerged from the Middle East and moved into Europe where they began to displace the Neanderthals about 30,000 years ago. Fossils also prove that much interbreeding occurred between Modern Man and Neanderthals up until 24,500 years ago.

Before the beginning of the fifth cycle, native humans had not been imprinted and were somewhat mentally blank. They lived throughout the Earth and were different colours, sizes and shapes. In Europe the race was about five feet tall, somewhat stocky, bow-legged, dark-haired, with heavy brow ridges and deep-set eyes. Not very intelligent, they resembled the images most people have of Neanderthals and, though hairier than us, they were not covered with hair.

Darker than the early Europeans, the people of Africa had curly hair and looked somewhat like the bushman of today. They were of slender build and had little body hair for they lived in a warmer country. Those of the East, referred to by archaeologists as Java man, had an oriental cast with a moon-shaped face and yellow skin. In North America the people had red skin, used bows and arrows and were meat-eaters. They lived in stone and wood shelters and used mud as cement between the rocks and wood. The tepee formation for shelter was actually shown to them by the Atlanteans.

There were also green humans that had descended directly from Lemurians. Legends of mermaids and various fish gods derive from our collective unconscious about these beings. Ancient Sumeria and Babylon had a fish god called Oannes, who was beneficent as many of the green humans were. Oannes was depicted with a human head and torso and with fish-like legs and feet.

During the fifth cycle, the green humans lived on the south-eastern shore of the Mediterranean in the Middle East. But even then they were dying out. They had webbed feet and hands and spent most of their time in the water, although they slept, had their offspring, and built shelters on land. They used fire and were more intelligent than the native humans evolving on land, but they were more vulnerable to attack, as they could not move as quickly on land as the other humans. Being peaceful, they did not like conflict, which made it more difficult to defend themselves.

Pleiadians originally seeded the green humans just as Sirians seeded many Atlanteans. Both star systems worked co-operatively on developing humans. Pleiadians helped humans who lived in the water, as Pleiadians excel in their ability to develop the emotional body of Earth and its inhabitants. Sirians, on the other hand, excel in their development of the mental body, which was more developed in humans who lived on land. Both Sirians and Pleiadians interchanged their genes with members of the native human population to create hybrids and the green humans were these hybrids. Even in the present day some humans have genes descending from these green ones. Usually they do not look their age, are seldom ill, and when they die, it is most often of heart problems. Anwar Sadat, the former Egyptian president known for his peacekeeping efforts, was descended from these green human beings, as are many Bedouin.

The Atlanteans founded twelve main colonies whose purpose was to raise the consciousness of humans. Many aboriginal cultures speak of gods visiting them in flying crafts. These were Atlanteans, visiting the colonies in flying ships. Some enlightened Atlanteans were even able to materialize their bodies in places of their choosing, and these appearances were even more godlike. Atlanteans taught sciences, arts, language and mathematics to developing humans. The Egyptian gods Osiris and Isis, as mentioned previously, were Els from Sirius who had helped to develop the Atlantean culture. The Egyptians credited them with introducing grain, wine and many other civilizing items. Quetzalcoatl, who gave the Mayans the calendar, astronomical observatories, and laws about how to live, was also a Sirian who helped in Atlantis.

Atlanteans built their temples and shrines on the strong energy currents referred to as leylines of the Earth. They knew that anything built on these sites would retain their energy blueprint much longer. This has turned out to be true and many sacred sites, such as the Great Pyramid and Sphinx, still retain this energy to the present day. The Great Pyramid was built for many purposes. Its first and greatest purpose is as an electrical and magnetic charging device in the middle of the Earth, for it bisects the landmasses of the planet that are located at the centre of the Earth. The Pyramid is a homing device for sentient life forms coming to Earth from other solar systems and galaxies. It sends out a call that says, "This is Earth. We call you. We greet you. We bid you welcome."

The Great Pyramid is like a transmitting and receiving aerial whose frequencies resonate in the centre of the Earth. The beings of the inner Earth tap into this Pyramid's power to become aware of spacecraft that land, and to perceive what is happening both on and above the Earth's surface. This Pyramid was originally encased in crystalline stones that shone in the sunlight, amplifying energy. Remnants of these stones can still be seen near the cap. The pyramid form itself is based on consciousness. It absorbs the energy of the Sun and, using that energy, is able to receive and transmit communications.

The pyramid form has been important to many peoples. For example, Tibetans wear a pyramid-shaped hat to develop consciousness. Also, the Star of David can be used to form a six-pointed star in one's heart that is composed of pyramids. These pyramids are used to anchor the Creator's light and love through one's heart onto Earth and to take love from the Earth back up to the heavens.

Knowing the geometry and mathematics of divine laws, Atlantean colonists built the Great Pyramid. In the geometry of this Pyramid is the knowledge of the Earth, its place in this solar system and its relationship to other planets. The stones of the Pyramid were laid both by flying craft and by Atlanteans who were able to levitate them into place. Native humans worked on the site but not in the major part of the construction.

Within the Great Pyramid are chambers that were used to test individuals in the second, third and fourth levels of consciousness. The second took place in the queen's chamber. The third, which is attuned to open the solar plexus and to keep it open, occurred in the king's chamber. The fourth, which is attuned to the Sun/Son, took place in the exact middle of the Pyramid.

The Great Pyramid was not built to house dead pharaohs, and the solid piece of stone that is the sarcophagus found in the king's chamber is too large to go through the entrance to that room. It was, in fact, teleported there. The Great Pyramid itself is the greatest reading of the Book of Life. There are parts of the Great Pyramid that are unseen and unknown even today. Their doors open at night only to people who resonate at the appropriate frequencies. In the Great Pyramid the third dimensional reality overlaps with the Void and with other dimensions. At the time when the Pyramid was constructed, the Sons of the Gods, as the Atlanteans and later their descendants were called, had telepathy, levitation, and one-pointed thought to a degree that surpasses all one-pointed thought existent on Earth today. Even the powers of most yogis pale in comparison to the abilities of the ancient Egyptian ruling class.

When the Great Pyramid of Giza was built, the Sons of the Gods were still in control of Egypt. There were many hybrid humans on Earth by that time and the Sons of the Gods saw that their own race of beings would soon die out. They wished to build a landmark of their knowledge, not out of pride or arrogance, but so future generations of humanity would learn what they knew. The Great Pyramid is just this, a sturdy permanent form that is physically seen by all, yet whose inner significance is not seen by those who resonate at lower frequencies.

Like the Great Pyramid, the Mayan temples at Tulum and Chitchenitza in Central America were astronomical observatories attuned to higher frequencies. They also were landmarks indicating to the Sky Gods that intelligent beings lived in that place. In addition to these above-ground structures, there were also tunnels and chambers beneath the Earth at Giza, Tulum and Chitchenitza that entered the Void and other realities.

The Sphinx was built even earlier than the Great Pyramid. Egyptologist R. A. Schwaller de Lubicz in his book, *The Temple Within Man,* called attention to the erosion of the Sphinx and stated it was caused by water and not sand. This was only one of the many things that made Schwaller de Lubicz unpopular with his contemporaries because his findings flew in the face of previously accepted facts about Egyptian history. John Anthony West, author of *Serpent in the Sky,* took him seriously, hiring American geologist Robert Schoch, who did a computer analysis revealing that the Sphinx is indeed eroded by water. Schoch and West calculated that the Sphinx has to be at least 10,000 to 15,000 years old, perhaps older. This makes the Sphinx the oldest sculpture built on Earth. The Sphinx is in the desert, hardly a place for water damage. Could it be that the water damage happened at the time of the sinking of Atlantis?

Edgar Cayce, called the sleeping prophet, made countless predictions that have proved true. One of his predictions is that the lost records from Atlantis would be found between the paws of the Sphinx. Cayce could be speaking literally or his words could be a metaphor. The Sphinx and Great Pyramid are repositories of great knowledge with geometrical and archaeological complexity that are evident in their building. It is unlikely that the Atlanteans would go to the trouble of building monuments to last over 10,000 years if they were not to serve some purpose. I believe that when the time is right we will be able to decode the information that they have left to us.

Atlanteans ensured that their knowledge would be preserved in two other ways. The first was by teaching native humans, and this knowledge has come down to us as myths. Atlanteans knew that the survival of all they had achieved depended on the native human cultures carrying on their traditions. The timing for this was perfect, as the natives would not have been evolved enough prior to that time to benefit from what the Atlanteans had to offer. The Atlanteans informed the natives that they were Sons of the Gods who had been seeded on Earth by advanced beings from other stars. They told this in order to turn the attention of the native humans to the more evolved beings in other solar systems that they would one day meet in friendship.

A second way that Atlanteans raised the consciousness of developing humans was to interbreed with them, which created hybrids with suppler bodies and greater intelligence. These hybrids did not always survive, because genetically they were neither human nor Atlantean. Atlanteans sometimes married these hybrids, which developed more compassion, understanding, humility and love from sharing their essence with these developing humans. It was easier for Atlantean males to give their seed to humans than for an Atlantean female to carry a native child to term. As a result, Atlantean males fertilized greater numbers of humans.

Myths of various ancient cultures have recorded this process. For example, the Greek god Zeus was reputed to be a randy god who continually left his goddess wife Hera to chase after nymphs and humans from whom many children ensued. One of these children was Dionysus, the half-human half-god who was credited with bringing music and wine to the ancient Greeks. Zeus was an Atlantean—as were the entire pantheon of Greek gods—and Dionysus was his hybrid son. The worship of Dionysus is very old. His symbols are the goat and bull. The Age of the Goat is Capricorn, which began approximately 20,000 BCE, and the Age of the Bull is Taurus, which began around 4,000 BCE. The years between these dates are the years when Atlanteans and their descendants attempted to assist the native human population. The influence of the Atlantean colonists ended with the advent of the Arian Age. This is illustrated in the Old Testament of the Bible when Moses climbs Mount Sinai and is given a new set of laws for the Arian Age. He is horrified when he returns to the Israelites to see that they have relapsed into worshipping the calf, the symbol of a previous Taurian Age.

It was in accordance with the divine plan that Atlanteans and native humans would interbreed. The Atlanteans knew that their culture was doomed to die out and that their only chance of continuance was through these developing humans. Atlanteans sought to implant their wisdom in the physical, emotional and mental bodies of humans, so that humans would be the best and not the worst of what the Atlanteans had been.

We read an account of this time in the first six chapters of *Genesis*, "And it came to pass, when men began to multiply on the face of the Earth, and daughters were born unto them, that the sons of God saw the daughters of men, that they were fair; and they took them wives of all which they chose…There were giants on the Earth in those days and also after that; when the sons of God came into the daughters of men and they bore children to them, the same became mighty men which were of old, men of renown."

In India, the Atlanteans and their immediate descendents also intermarried with the natives, but some chose monastic lives and retreated into deep caves. In Tibet especially, humans living the life of a householder only met the monks who lived in the outer caves. These monks were not as enlightened as the ones in the inner caves. Some wise ones in the inner caves were unknown even to the monks in the outer caves. These wise ones lived for hundreds, even thousands, of years. They passed down their teachings to those in the inner caves who, in turn, passed on the teachings to monks in outer caves, who in turn passed it on to less spiritually advanced humans who were able to absorb some of it. This practice also occurred in the Andes of South America. Wise ones chose to live at high altitudes on Earth because it is easier to access higher spiritual dimensions where the ethers are less cluttered with the thoughts of multitudes of people and where the air carries a higher frequency of energy.

In the second half of the fifth cycle, the sons of the Gods dwindled in population and were dying out on Earth. The sons of the Gods had developed their astral body and heart chakra because of their devotion to others, and this development was inherited by their successors. Hybrids rose in population because of their intelligence and consciousness and became much as they are today. Some primitive natives still roamed wild, but they, too, were becoming extinct. It was the hybrids, and those who interacted with the hybrids, who evolved. The lineage of the Atlanteans became weaker as their hybrids bred with other hybrids and then those hybrids bred with pure native stock. Even today, there are a few pure sons of the Gods still existent on Earth who are able to materialize and dematerialize their form. They are great teachers who have ascended, but who return to help us.

The fifth cycle of evolution saw the development of colonies, the heart chakra and the astral realm. Learning to help others, with science, mathematics and human law aligned to divine law.

A question that I am sometimes asked is, "How do you know this information and how can I access it as well?" I believe that this information is available to everyone as their frequency increases. I have found that when early phases of my own evolution become relevant in my present life, I remember them. Likewise, I recall the collective evolution of humanity when it is of use to do so. This information is available to each of us in the Akashic Records and it is our divine inheritance, our birthright, to access both our personal past lives and also the records of our collective history on Earth. Most of us have had many incarnations on Earth. Some of these are more significant than others in understanding relationships, roles and the purpose for our present life. I offer you a guided visualization exercise that you might find helpful to explore one of your most significant lives.

Exercise 15: Experience a Past Life

Take a moment to still your mind before doing the following visualization. You may want to read the questions before starting, or record yourself reading the questions and then play them back, or enlist a friend to read them to you.

Go to a private, quiet place and close your eyes....See a doorway that opens to your present life and open it. You enter a corridor with doors on each side. Ask yourself, "Which door is the entrance to a significant past life that would be helpful for me to see today?" When you receive your answer, walk through that door. (Pause to receive answers after each question).

- ❖ What is the first thing you see?

- ❖ Look at your feet and notice what is on them...your hands... how are you dressed? Look at your face and notice your eyes... hair? Are you a man or woman? How old are you?

- ❖ Go to the place where you lived in that life. What does the building look like?

- ❖ Imagine sitting down for an evening meal. What are you eating?

- ❖ Is anyone eating with you? If so, what is your relationship with this person? He or she may look different, but do you recognize this person in your present life? If so, what is your relationship now and how does your past relationship impact your present one?

- ❖ See yourself doing the work you do in that life. What is it? Is there anything similar to what you do in your current life?

- ❖ What was the purpose of that life? How does this purpose relate to your present life?

- ❖ Is there any other question that you would like to ask about that life? If so, you will hear or see the answer now.

Remember all that you learned in this visualization. Take a moment to reflect on the answers before opening your eyes and record what you learned in your journal.

Historical Age: The Sixth Cycle

The fifth cycle—The Age of Greek, Scandinavian and Indian Gods who were the Atlanteans—was a cycle of prehistory and myth for humanity. With the end of this fifth cycle, we entered a time of recorded history, commencing with the Egyptian, Minoan, and Indian cultures. At approximately 4,000 BCE the sixth great cycle of our evolution began; it continues into the present day.

The sixth cycle has witnessed humanity's growth in intellectual achievements and technology. Over this last six thousand years, humans have been completing the development of their lower mental body, centred in their solar plexus, and their free will, ego, and sense of "I, me, mine." This has increased our independence from the group and our desire to increase our personal value and wealth. With an increased value put on accumulating inorganic things, such as money, houses, TV's, cars, there has been a decreased value of organic life, including other people, the natural environment, and spirituality.

People have become objects to which breast implants, face-lifts, and other people's organs can be added. Professions assisting people, such as teaching, child raising, and social work, have much less status and are less rewarded than professions such as banking and corporate business that generate money and things. Animals, water, trees, and air have no value of themselves, their value being seen only in how much money can be gained in their sale. World leaders support wars that kill hundreds of thousands of people annually leaving famine and death of more thousands in their wake.

Has any good emerged from the sixth cycle of human evolution? Yes, we have developed our free will, made choices, and developed a strong lower mental body. Now we are learning through pain what not to do. As discontent with the present system increases, individuals and groups will create new systems based on organic principles based on divine law, which will be the foremost principle of the seventh cycle of human evolution. However, before that can transpire we need to go through the last major phase of the sixth cycle—the information age.

On the positive side, with the recent activation of the etheric template in the throat chakra, the information age has been born that links all beings on the Earth and to the Earth simultaneously. This web makes communication possible instantaneously where satellites see you and your home from space. The use of the etheric template, centred in the throat chakra, allows us to reprogram the world and ourselves. This will come to fruition in the seventh great cycle of humanity, which is just now commencing on Earth.

As you have seen, the cycles become shorter as the Earth and humans evolve. These later cycles last only thousands of years whereas the first two cycles took millions of years. Cycles overlap each other. One cycle starts to wane as another one starts to grow. At this time the majority of people are anchored in the sixth cycle of human evolution, but some individuals are starting the seventh. This is occurring simultaneously. Still other individuals have not yet completed the earlier cycles. This is true of the oldest peoples on Earth—the bushman of Africa and Australian aboriginals. However, aboriginal groups have members who are in the sixth and seventh cycles of evolution, who are wayshowers for their people.

Many pure aboriginals have gifts of the dreamtime and clairvoyance, which have been lost to humans in later cycles. Talents are seemingly lost in each cycle, but they are absorbed as a kind of psychic food to feed individuals in the next cycle. This is in accordance with divine law, for if we depend on old gifts, we never learn new ones. The best of the preceding age is brought into the following age. This principle is very like what happens to a caterpillar that dies to its former life to become a butterfly. In fact, it does not die in its cocoon state, but absorbs the best of its caterpillar state to feed its transformation into a butterfly.

Each of these seven cycles in human evolution has a group soul. Although individual members of a soul group might ascend whenever he or she has learned the appropriate lessons, the soul group itself might not yet have ascended. It is hoped that the seventh cycle will accelerate the growth and learning of the humans of the other cycles. Too many individuals of the third, fourth, and fifth cycles still lag behind seeking power, status, and money. These people are trapped in illusion and attachments, which are like an infectious disease from which it is difficult to recover once one has succumbed. It is possible for a person to be almost free of attachments and then to have a relapse, which sets him or her back thousands of years in evolution. This has happened with many of those in the third and fourth cycle.

Many ascended members of the third, fourth, and fifth cycles have reincarnated to help humans of other cycles complete their evolution. It takes a shorter period of time for individuals in the sixth cycle to complete their evolution for two reasons. First, they begin with more consciousness because they were with the Creator for a longer time prior to incarnating than the individuals of the preceding cycles. Furthermore, they have the advantage of the cumulative wisdom of the individuals who preceded them.

The sixth cycle of evolution, our current historical age, awakens the solar plexus and throat. It features intellectual and technological achievements, working on the lower mental/etheric template.

Enlightened Humans: The Seventh Cycle

The seventh cycle of human evolution is that of the enlightened human. During this period, we will learn control of the higher mental body. The throat and crown chakras will become more active as we enter higher frequencies. This will take the form of communicating, once again, with beings on higher levels of consciousness. Angels, Ascended Masters from human evolution and Els are included here. Our communication will be very different from the way we communicated in the third and fourth cycles of Lemuria and Atlantis. During that time, humans were like little children who were told by these spiritual guardians what to do, and we did it. We did not think for ourselves. Our lessons were to learn obedience to divine law through trust in others.

Now, we enter the seventh cycle to learn partnership and co-creation. Our guardians have been witnessing human experiments with creation for thousands of years. When we work with higher spiritual principles, we receive energy from our guardians to further our development. This energy, or prana, is a kind of food that feeds and grows our higher spiritual bodies. Through this process we have evolved to the point where we are young adults ready to be employed in our first job as world servers on Earth.

During the seventh cycle, the majority of humans will move to the fourth level of consciousness as the Earth does likewise. Our life theme will become co-creation with divine law on Earth. Humans will become conscious guardians for lower evolutions—the mineral, plant, fish, bird, and animal kingdoms. We will be safe, having overcome the dangers of destroying others and ourselves through greed, fear, and other negative emotions. Consequently, the ring-pass-not that separates Earth from other planets and solar systems will be removed. This will allow us to communicate with beings from the stars, some of which have been observing our progress and even helping us. The rise in interest in channelling, astrology, altered states of consciousness, UFOs, as well as science fiction and fantasy in literature and film, are harbingers of meeting these others.

This does not mean that humans will be perfect. We will still be learning many lessons. For example, learning how to shepherd other Earth species will not be easy. It will be tempting to do things "for their own good." We might think that we know better than them, and some of us will have to learn not to blow dry the budding flowers to make them bloom faster. Another challenge will be to surrender attachment to our racial, national, and religious identities. Why is this necessary? Because it's the first step in becoming world citizens. Having accomplished this, the next step is to overcome our identification with our planet so we can become galactic citizens.

Many themes of the seventh cycle are emerging even today. Sustainability in all forms will be key. Alternative energy systems based on wind, water, and solar power will replace the use of oil and gas. Organic food, composting, nurturing the soil will replace the use of insecticides, pesticides, and steroids, and we will consume less meat and more fish, fruit, and grains. We will begin living from the energy of the sun and this will increase in later cycles of our evolution. Healing will be less invasive as we move from cut and stitch to prevention of illness. We will use plants and homeopathic remedies to restore balance as opposed to the heavy use of numbing pharmaceuticals that we used during the sixth cycle.

Based on knowledge found in subatomic quantum physics, the ruling paradigm will become an awareness that we create our own reality. The primary way of altering our world will be by changing our values, which will change our thoughts, behaviour and therefore reality. This process will happen on all levels, with individuals, groups, and large governing systems. With this change in thinking individuals will no longer believe in scarcity and those with more will give to those who have less. This means there will no longer be the poverty and starvation that we have seen in earlier cycles.

In the sixth cycle we learned what not to do, and in the seventh cycle humanity will learn what to do in order to create with divine laws. Leaders in the seventh cycle will be those whose values do not conform to the dominant paradigm in today's world. Those who have the power today will find it most difficult to change, as they might feel they will lose everything they have gained. Yet individuals do change when the pain of not changing is greater than the pain of changing.

Let's examine a second process through which this transformation occurs. Seventh cycle children choose highly developed parents of sixth and sometimes fourth, or fifth, cycles. The Karmic Board, comprised of members of human and other evolutions, determines the exact genetic and spiritual makeup that would allow each individual to make the most gains in a lifetime. This is a complex process. As individuals evolve to higher levels of consciousness they need highly evolved bodies capable of holding their soul energy. Sometimes it is difficult to find parents to host these evolved individuals. What complicates this situation even more is that many spiritually evolved people decide not to have children. This results in fewer parents available with the frequency necessary to host highly evolved children of any cycle.

Why would spiritually evolved individuals decide not to have children when they know that their bodies are needed? It is because their primary commitment is to serve those who have already incarnated. These individuals have often taken the Bodhisattva vow to remain on Earth until all humans are ascended, so they are committed to developing consciousness with large numbers of people. As you know, it takes approximately 18 years to raise a child. During this time, the primary commitment of parents, and of women especially, goes into parenting that child. Consequently, their energy is not as available to help a larger number of people. This is a major reason many women on a spiritual path decide not to have children. Previously, it was not as difficult for men, who traditionally had not been the primary caregivers. However, this is changing, as more men are making joint parenting a reality in our society.

For a similar reason, some women do not have partners. By doing so, the temptation to give their love to only one person is removed. Many spiritual individuals do not know that this is the agreement they have made with the Karmic Board before incarnating. After incarnating, the joys of partnership or parenting become very appealing and they would like to have that experience. It might not happen, however, because this was not their pre-arranged agreement. The result is that many spiritual women doing great good in helping the world, may find themselves alone. Examining this situation on the personality level it doesn't make sense to see dedicated women with such sadness. Yet on the higher soul level this situation is absolutely right. This can also be the case with men but it is rarer due to cultural norms and gender differences. For instance, men more often place their work in the world ahead of relationship.

Some individuals of the seventh cycle have already ascended although they have only just commenced their Earth incarnations. These people will reincarnate again and again to assist members in all cycles to become conscious co-creators. Jesus says of them, "Whosoever shall humble himself as this little child, the same is the greatest in the Kingdom of Heaven." The child of whom Jesus speaks is a Bodhisattva and there are Bodhisattva individuals in all seven cycles.

The seventh cycle will complete a certain state in human evolution. It will link the third dimensional reality of the material world to the fourth dimension and other realities. Individuals of the seventh cycle who are presently incarnating are the bravest of their soul group, as the Earth is still not fully prepared to nurture humans of their cycle. They are pure beings who are open in the crown chakra. As children many of these are strong willed, outspoken, insightful beyond their years, and able to know if others are speaking the truth or not. In school, some are very gifted while others might be hyperactive or bored as the system does not teach the way in which they learn. Because seventh cycle children are so open to higher spiritual principles and realms, it is difficult presently for them to live in the third dimension on Earth because of the negativity. These seventh cycle individuals will influence others for the good. These are called the Indigo children, as indigo is the colour of the ray on which they are incarnating. Some of these children incarnate for only a few years in this lifetime, just long enough to open their parents to love, light and joy.

Such seventh cycle individuals, incarnating now, are lighting the path for the majority who will soon follow. These seventh cycle individuals help to raise humanity to the fourth dimension, where the majority of our evolution in the next cycle will take place. However, there is much cleansing of the Earth that needs to happen before this transpires; a cleansing that will occur in both the third and fourth dimensions. By the end of the seventh cycle, all members of humanity will be committed to co-creation with divine law. Humans will then be able to work in the fifth dimension with beings of higher consciousness.

As our mental, emotional, physical and etheric bodies develop, we assume more responsibility for our thoughts, feelings and actions. We have less room for error and are more accountable because we are more conscious of how we affect others. Development through the cycles has led hundreds of thousands of individuals to the brink of full spiritual transformation. During the next two thousand years humanity will make a quantum leap in consciousness as more people awaken. We will then all live in accordance with divine law.

During this transitional period, it will become more obvious that there are two, and not one, prevailing value systems. The first is the dominant law of our nation, which is the lower law of our personality that makes us safe in our relationships with others. Once we learn these laws, we enter a period of questioning to ascertain if these laws are in accordance with divine law and our soul's purpose in life. A time of inner and even outer conflict might arise as we decide to follow higher spiritual laws and not national laws that disagree with higher ones.

Gandhi displayed these difficulties when he chose not to pay the British salt tax and encouraged others to do the same. This action was against the law of his country and yet, it was in accordance with a higher law of home rule. It resulted in the end of colonialism in India. We see examples of people living by higher laws demonstrated in every walk of life today. Many are antiwar demonstrators, animal rights activists, environmental advocates, and spokespeople for equal rights for all races, genders and ages. Some people might be imprisoned for their actions as they are illegal by their country's standards, and yet they are the vanguard of where our world will move during this seventh cycle.

We must be patient and tolerant during this time of transition. We cannot speed up the process, as individuals come to recognize the difference between lower and higher laws. In Lemuria and Atlantis, the Laggards force-fed developing humans free will before these early humans were ready to assume responsibility for their actions. That led to hundreds of thousands of years of retrograde behaviour from which we are only now emerging. Let us not repeat this mistake. We can all learn discernment about what food to offer people that would nourish them. To feed babies solid food before they learn to eat pureed vegetables is criminal, as they cannot digest it.

Some individuals have the desirable ability to work with people of all levels of consciousness. Mother Theresa, for example, in her work with the dying, opened the hearts of us all as she demonstrated the path of service. Others, like the Dalai Lama, are remarkable in knowing what to say to which audience. The Dalai Lama, appearing on *Larry King Live,* laughed about his earlier desire to be an engineer and describes himself as "just a simple monk." Yet, to his Tibetan followers and Buddhist colleagues, the Dalai Lama is an enlightened being. Both views are correct and he can be a friend along the path to both groups.

Discernment, which is the ability to know what is appropriate in each situation, is not a product of our lower, but of our higher mental body, and even of our higher causal/soul body. Let's examine how the higher mind develops so we can co-operate with the process. When we attend traditional schools, we are judged by how well we retain the information that we are taught. We are viewed as more intelligent if we have a good memory and are able to repeat our teacher's words by rote. Memorizing information is more of a left-brain function employed by the lower mind. Some information however, such as spiritual ideas, might seem elusive because it lies in the realm of the higher mind. The laws that control the higher mind are different from the laws for the lower mind, and the laws for working with the physical and emotional bodies are different again.

To control our lower mental body, we explore ideas and concepts, learn to analyze pros and cons, and solve problems using available data. With our lower mind we acquire knowledge. We reach out in a more yang way and grasp with the mind. This is the antithesis of what is needed to develop the higher mind. If we try to learn higher spiritual concepts in an intellectual way we impede our progress. To develop the higher mind we need to allow the information to settle in us. This is a yin function. Let's use a metaphor of seeing a pebble drop into the water and watching the ripples extending out. These ripples are how the higher mind works. There is a series of oscillations that bring the mind into a harmonious frequency with all that is known. The lower mind, by contrast, works not with the whole mind but in little pieces and sections that are isolated from the whole.

Qualities of Higher and Lower Mind

Higher Mind	Lower Mind
Yin	Yang
Wisdom reveals itself	Acquire knowledge
Harmonious resonance	Isolated pieces
Inner knowing	Analysis
Being	Doing

Figure 9 - This chart can assist with recognition of aspects of mind function.

We must often unlearn what we have previously learned in order to move to a higher frequency. At first glance this might appear like senility, menopause, or burnout. However, it is an evolutionary process. Reading this book, or any spiritual book that works with the higher mental body, will transform you by creating a resonance in your higher mental body. Just as chanting holy words, which are not in our language, works regardless of whether we fully understand them or not, so higher spiritual truths work upon you if your bodies are developed sufficiently to resonate with them. Transformation is ongoing. The spiritual teacher Ram Dass has shared instances from his own life that help us to understand this process.

As a young Harvard professor, Ram Dass experimented liberally, and that's an understatement, with LSD. After many years, he discontinued its use because he discovered that in his everyday life he was not able to sustain the spiritual truths that he had observed while using LSD. His desire for spirit took him to India where he committed to the teacher Neem Karoli Baba. Through being in the presence of this enlightened Master, Ram Dass and thousands of others were able to maintain higher frequencies of love and unity with the Divine than they could do on their own or by using drugs. This is the power of studying with a spiritual teacher. Going from teacher to teacher is more like taking drugs. We might have stimulating ah ha's, but we cannot maintain this condition on our own. Only through meditation, studying spiritual truths, and being in the presence of someone who resonates at higher frequencies will we be able to stay in higher levels of consciousness.

As higher frequencies increase in our bodies, they interfere with lower inharmonious frequencies created by erroneous thoughts, feelings, and actions. When this happens, an inner conflict for dominance is created between our personality and soul. Rather than contracting and becoming more rigid by trying to figure everything out, it's preferable to relax with the information and allow it to unfold in us. In other words, expand, don't contract, through this process. The higher mental body is not so much interested in the right answer; it wants us to sense an inner knowing that is often beyond words.

Since I was a child my higher mind has been stronger than my lower mind. That might seem like the desirable goal but I can assure you it was difficult for me growing up. Because of this I had great difficulty in school memorizing the streams of information that I was supposed to know to echo back during exams. Also, occasionally I appeared obstinate to teachers when I knew something was incorrect that was being stated, although the teacher assured me that the facts were correct. The solution was to strengthen my lower mind and I learned to quote scientific facts to support my knowing that came from my higher mind. This allowed me to be more acceptable in the way that our material world currently views intelligence.

Exercise 16: Qualities of Your Higher and Lower Mind

Take time to still your mind before answering the following questions and record your observations in your journal.

❖ List qualities that you associate with the lower mind.

❖ Which qualities of your lower mind do you use to be successful in the world?

❖ Which qualities of the lower mind do you want to develop?

❖ How will you develop these qualities of the lower mind?

❖ List the qualities you associate with the higher mind.

❖ What qualities of the higher mind do you want to develop?

❖ How will you develop these qualities of the higher mind?

Section Four

OTHER SPECIES EVOLVING ON THE EARTH

Gift from a Hummingbird

As dusk approaches
hummingbirds rush the feeder
gathering reserves for the night.

Quietly I slip closer
placing my fingers under the flowers,
completely still, hardly daring to breathe,
I wait.

Soon a buzz draws near.
A living jewel alights on my finger
inches from my face sucking the sweet nectar,
flooding my heart with joy.

Elementals

As we resonate in higher frequencies, which will happen to humanity in the seventh cycle of our evolution, we realize that we are the guardians of many species including animals, birds, plants, and minerals. We also become aware of other sentient beings who are evolving on the Earth. One of these elementals, also called nature spirits. They exist in a slightly higher dimension with a faster frequency than the world in which the majority of humans live. Just as a piano has both white and black keys, which represent dominant and half-tones, so there are half-tones between dimensions. Humans are conscious in the third dimension, which is a dominant major key. The elementals live in a dimension a half-tone higher than ours, which is in a minor key.

Because we are able to physically see insects, birds, animals and fish, it is easier to understand our relationship with them than with elementals. Elementals and humans, however, have the greatest potential to interact and help each other than any other species on Earth. Elementals are native to the planet and we have gone through the various cycles of evolution together. Actually, humans already know a great deal about them from myths of various cultures. Earth elementals, such as leprechauns, gnomes, brownies, trolls and elves, are easiest for us to see and interact with, as their frequency, being the heaviest, is closest to that of humans.

Humans interacted more with elementals in the past when we lived closer to the land and were more in harmony with nature. With the advent of the industrial age, most people lost that connection, but there is currently a marked renewal of interest in elementals throughout the world. This interest is closely aligned with our desire to reconnect with the Earth. It is part of the divine plan that humans and elementals work together to create on this planet, with humans creating the vision and elementals manifesting it. Therefore, it is essential that we learn more about their evolution and how we can work co-operatively with them.

The word *elemental* evokes for some people an image of little one-inch fairies who hop from flower to flower making them grow. Fairies are less evolved elementals, the equivalent of chimpanzees being precursors of humans. There are many kinds of elementals including *undines* that work with water, *sylphs* who work with air, and *salamanders* that work with fire. Elementals range in size from the minute life force found in subatomic particles to great *devas* of weather systems and mountain ranges. Because the evolution of water, air and fire elementals is very different from that of humans, we more commonly interact with earth elementals, which we'll discuss here.

Elementals have a corporal form, intelligence, and consciousness. They encompass a larger range of physical forms than do humans. The form they choose to present to us may be thin, delicately boned, with slanted and intense eyes, pointed ears and a triangular-shaped face. Their physical form is much lighter and of a faster frequency than ours. These beings are visible to humans most often in the etheric realm, which in metaphysical literature is often referred to as the subtle physical body.

Elementals are developing their emotional body and actually work through this body to manifest what they want in the world. Since they are not developing the heart centre in the same way as humans, they are not subjected to the same pressures. At this time in elemental evolution, their mental body is not as developed as that of humans. Humans know more than elementals about the power of one-pointed thought and concentration. However, most humans do not consciously make use of this power. Elementals are able to materialize objects on their etheric plane more easily than humans can on the physical plane. Very few elementals are able to materialize in our physical dimension, which is presently too heavy for them, and this is why humans seldom see them.

Elementals do not have free will as humans do. Among the beings that left the Creator's heart, humans have gone a very long way on the road to independence. Elementals have not gone nearly as far, and have never left the realms of beautiful music, colour and smell. Their evolutionary destiny was not for them to become co-creators with free will like humans, but instead to work in partnership with us and other evolving co-creators. This plan was altered in the last several hundred years when humans abandoned this partnership. Some elementals are now working with their equivalent of the Karmic Board to learn how to become creators with free will and have sought out humans with whom to partner in this endeavour. These numbers will grow during the seventh cycle of human evolution, however, let's speak of the norm in this current time.

Earth elementals—those working most closely with humans—have a hereditary, graduated caste system. These castes are divided into kings, princes, nobles, and various craft guilds. These craft guilds specialize in colour, sound, aroma, and working with the elements of air, fire, water and earth. Included in these castes are hunters, musicians, legend weavers, clothiers, storytellers, artists, magicians, healers and warriors. Each elemental caste has a specific purpose that is instinctive to its nature to accomplish. Elementals, unlike humans, do not think in terms of wanting to change jobs.

Some elementals live for hundreds of years, and in rare instances over a thousand. Elementals start their evolution hollow and as they mature from lifetime to lifetime, their hollowness disappears. Their bodies are vital forces of energy and light, which is divine fire, and they bring light wherever they walk. Humans evolve in just the opposite way. We start full of the earth element and hollow ourselves by use of the fire of the Holy Spirit.

Elementals believe in a supreme power that controls all things and that creates all beauty. As humans have lives of learning, elementals have lives filled with beauty and joy. Also, their memory is not the same as ours. They see everything in the constant now, unlike humans who divide time into past, present and future.

Elementals are aware of other evolutions, such as animal and human, and their healing caste, in particular, wishes to bring these other evolutions into harmony with divine law. Elementals do not attempt to change others but rather to assist the true, highest essence of the individual to manifest. Physical, emotional and mental disharmony in humans is poison to elementals and they might attempt to restore us to harmony. They do not help out of personal interest or compassion, but because it's their purpose.

The elemental world has a Moon, Sun and Earth, but these exist in a different dimension than ours. During the days and nights of the full Moon the doors are open between the elemental and human kingdoms, and during the solstices and equinoxes the doors are open even wider. Humans and elementals are able to cross into each other's worlds in locations where the veils are thin. Pollution does not exist in their world and when humans raise their frequency to higher levels of consciousness pollution will not exist for us either.

There are highly evolved elementals—like the human equivalent of the Masters—who are members of the hierarchy for the Earth. Pan, the mythic half-goat and half-human being, is the head of elemental evolution. He works under the auspices of Buddha, as do all evolving species on Earth. Buddha heads all evolutions because only one who has complete free will, as those of human evolution have, can be Lord of this World. Humanity has a greater struggle than other Earth species in fulfilling its purpose, but once it is achieved, it will be able to create for the entire Earth. Elementals have less free will and do not evolve the same qualities of creation as we do.

Els entered elemental evolution to assist them in developing their curiosity, consciousness and love of learning. These Els shared their genetic material with elementals even as they did with humans. There is a close bond between elementals and Els as the strength of both races is in creating form. Some Els succumbed to the temptations of elemental life, after which they had to evolve out of elemental evolution.

Some evolved elementals have entered human evolution to learn free will to assist with the development of elementals and other beings. In order to do this, an elemental must have developed a strong ego body so he, or she, will not be swayed by the strong will of humans. Humanity has benefited from this process that is sanctioned by the elemental equivalent of the Karmic Board.

Vincent Van Gogh, for example, was originally from elemental evolution and his art was a great gift to humanity. Some of his gifts and difficulties are typical of elemental hybrids. Van Gogh had the mental instability that accompanies elemental evolution. Also, he could see and hear things that humans could not and these characteristics helped him to become a great painter. Van Gogh entered human evolution to develop free will and he exerted his will in many ways, even in his decision to take his own life. This was unfortunate, as divine law does not sanction suicide, although for elementals death is a much easier process than it is for humans. Elementals only need to think of going into the Void and it happens. Dying is a fading from one reality into another and elementals can choose to do this without negating divine law. Van Gogh's life demonstrates the difficulties that occur when a being crosses from one evolution to another and transposes the laws of two separate evolutions.

Both elementals and humans are curious and love to experience new things, and this is one of their attractions to the other's evolution. It is rare for human Masters to enter the elemental realm after their ascension, but humans occasionally do before then. It is more common for elementals to enter human evolution at the elemental equivalent of the ascension, as some believe that they can better serve their race as full co-creators.

Time in the elemental world is different from time in the human one. Humans have visited the elemental kingdom for what they thought to be days or months only to return to the human world and discover that their families had died of old age. As elementals age, they retain their physical beauty, whereas aging humans, even while in the elemental world, have grey hair and become saggy. Elementals do not find elderly humans attractive, and elementals entering human evolution often find it traumatic to lose their physical beauty.

There are many disincentives to crossing into each other's worlds. Yet it can be done. There are places on Earth that are points of crossing, such as Avebury in Great Britain. Stonehenge was a point of crossing in the past, but it no longer is. However, in Wales and Ireland there are still sacred caves and stone circles where one can cross. To do this, humans must be able to change their polarity and increase their frequency to that of the elemental world.

Elementals do not have the same moral and ethical code as humans. Through human eyes, they are often seen as cold-hearted and lacking compassion. Music, sound, colour, light, smell and movement are far more evolved in elementals than in us. For example, their music moves like the wind and water and is a more true reflection of nature than humans are able to create. Elementals move with a grace that humans do not have, and they see differently and more intensely. The world is much more alive for them and they have greater depth perception, both by day and night, than humans. Elementals retain more consciousness from life to life than humans, and, as mentioned previously, their lives are longer.

Because of these talents, elemental hybrids are drawn to the arts of music, poetry, dance and painting in the human world. They might also be drawn to alcohol, drugs, sex, and other ways of changing their reality, as they dislike the fixed form of the human world where they cannot create varied realities by thought alone.

Elementals enter human evolution to develop their heart chakra, specifically the three-fold flame of love, wisdom and divine will that resides there. These three qualities must be developed for beings to use free will and, as elementals have less free will than humans, they need to develop these.

Ways and places to cross between the elemental and human worlds were once more abundant than they are presently, however they are increasing again during this next two thousand years. This process has already commenced. Humans in their dream state are able to visit elementals for two reasons. Firstly, elementals sleep very little and secondly, they are conscious in their dreams, as humans will learn to be. In addition, as humans develop more acute perception of the subtle realms of existence, they are able to see elementals.

For the last century, rather than incarnating in human evolution, some elementals have chosen another option in order to learn free will. Highly developed elementals from all castes around the world are seeking humans with whom to work. Through working together to create a more beautiful and healthy planet, these elementals develop their free will and a stronger ego body without the risk of entering human evolution. This process has been very successful.

Many years ago I lived in a cottage on the west coast of Ireland that was inhabited by a leprechaun family. These leprechauns belonged to this group of elementals that wanted to co-create with humans and they asked me to assist them. I have done this by writing two books *Summer with the Leprechauns* and *Pilgrimage with the Leprechauns* and by offering workshops to people who wish to work with elementals. Just as we have a guardian angel, many of us have elementals who wish to be our friend. Many imaginary childhood play friends were really elementals who we learned not to see as we grew older. The story of Peter Pan, an elf living in Neverneverland, is a story of this.

The following visualization will help you to connect with an elemental friend that you can work with.

Exercise 17: Meet Your Elemental Friend

Take a moment to still your mind before doing the following visualization. You may want to read the questions before starting, or record yourself reading the questions and then play them back, or enlist a friend to read them to you.

Go to a private, quiet place and close your eyes....Imagine that you are in your favourite place in nature...You can see another being approaching. Welcome this being. (Pause to receive answers after each question).

❖ How is he, or she, dressed? Notice the eyes and hair.

❖ Ask your elemental friend what kind of elemental he, or she, is and have no preconceptions about what the response will be?

❖ Ask your friend what he, or she, is here to teach you?

❖ Ask your friend what you can teach him, or her?

❖ Your friend will give you a gift. Hold out your hand to receive it. What is it?

❖ Does your elemental friend want a gift from you? If you are able to do so, give it.

❖ Sometimes an elemental will give you his, or her, name. Ask what it is.

❖ Is there any other question that you would like to ask your elemental friend? If so, you will hear, or see, the answer now.

❖ Thank your elemental friend for coming and ask how and where you can contact him, or her, again.

Remember all that you learned in this visualization. Take a moment to reflect on the answers before opening your eyes and record what you learned in your journal.

The Body Elemental

Elementals not only share our planet, they also share our bodies. Each living being has a *body elemental*, and no life from the smallest atom to the greatest being can exist without it. A body elemental is a member of the elemental kingdom and it has a very specialized function with our etheric body. Individuals more often understand the functions of their physical, astral and mental bodies before learning about the function of their etheric body.

The Karmic Board gives the body elemental the memory of all creation, the species of its host, and instructions on building a body for each individual. The body elemental is the framework around which all else is built. It is also an architect that builds each of us according to a specific blueprint. These blueprints are the physical, emotional, mental, and causal/soul bodies of its host.

The body elemental is with us through all lives. It stores our karmic memory in our personal Book of Life in the Akashic Records. Reading these records, the Karmic Board that oversees our evolution is able to assess our weaknesses and our strengths. From this, it chooses the parents and set of environmental circumstances that will allow us to fulfil our life purpose. Often we reincarnate in certain soul groups because, having known these people before, we are better attuned to their essence and resonance. It is easier to work together with them than to start again with new people. This becomes more important the further we evolve, particularly after we have repaid any karma to them or them to us. In providing this record-keeping service, the body elemental also functions as a librarian.

In between incarnations of its host, the body elemental rests. First, it downloads all that it has learned into the Book of Life. Then the body elemental rejoins its soul group and adds what it has learned to the collective knowledge of these elementals. It takes up its function again when its host reincarnates.

As with other elementals, the body elemental does not have free will. Its evolution is totally linked to that of its host and it develops as its host develops in consciousness. Gradually over lifetimes, and working both with the Karmic Board and its host, it builds the vessel that allows its host to become enlightened. When this transpires, the body elemental is free to continue its evolution as a conscious being.

The memory of the body elemental remains with the host and, from that memory, the host is able to consciously rebuild his, or her, body by accessing the blueprint from the Akashic Records.

The body elemental controls all our bodily functions such as breathing, heartbeat, sleeping, orgasm and hunger. It controls these and many more instinctive functions. To evolve we learn to control these functions consciously with the assistance of the body elemental, who is then relieved to be freed of this work. The body elemental also helps us to control the elements in our bodies, teaching us to regulate the appropriate amounts of air, water, fire and earth. When we are able to do this within ourselves, we can then learn to employ this power in our outside world to light fires, bring rain, and dissolve clouds. A higher knowledge of the same principle leads to the ability to de-manifest and re-manifest the body, levitation, etc. We worked with the body elemental in Atlantean times to do many of these things, however our conscious connection was lost through the dominance of the ego, which does not want to share control with anything.

The body elemental, under the unconscious command of the ego, has built a strong vessel—the personality for the majority of humans. At this point in our evolution, it is necessary to resume conscious communication with the body elemental to de-manifest all the belief systems and negative emotions that are counterproductive to our continuing growth. As we continue this process of de-manifestation, the personality vessel is able to hold more of our soul, which can be used as the water of life to feed others.

We do not want to damage our vessel through this transformation process. This can happen through excessive fasting, flagellation, and denial of the body in a misguided attempt to serve spirit. These actions damage our body elemental when, instead, it deserves our gratitude. To love our body we need to give it good food, lots of hugs and joy and to treat it in the same way we would treat our own child. Many people, through abuse and negation of the body either in this or in past lives, have damaged their relationship with their body elemental. Just as a child might not trust an abusive parent, we need to heal the relationship through consistent efforts to think, feel and act positively towards our body. Also, as we think well of other sentient beings, these emotions create a positive relationship with our body elemental.

The Earth also has a body elemental, which holds the memories of all the mineral, plant, animal, human, and other kingdoms. This is a great task and one for which there is little acknowledgement although it takes eons for the body elemental of the Earth to accomplish this. Just as we must heal our relationship with our individual body elemental, we need to rebuild our relationship with the body elemental of the Earth. The way to do this is identical to that used in healing ourselves. We engage in this task as we move into the third and fourth levels of consciousness.

It is important to work closely with our body elemental in order to become a conscious creator. Jesus the Christ, for one, worked fully with his body elemental when he was able to manifest a physical body after death and transport to many locations. Before we get to that stage we need to work with our body elemental to heal physical illnesses and outmoded emotional and mental patterns that might stem from this or other lives.

I would like to share with you a personal story of working with my body elemental. Earlier in my life I had endometriosis. The cure usually involves laser surgery and, if this does not work, a hysterectomy. Preferring not to engage in either of these treatments I asked my body elemental about the cause of my endometriosis. It told me that I had a woman's body that grieved my decision not to have children so my body had grown the endometriosis inappropriately in my womb. Knowing the source of the difficulty I could then look for a solution. I asked my body if it would allow me to love other children and also postpone my own child bearing until my next life. It agreed and I was able to see my endometriosis cured and within a few weeks it was.

Exercise 18: Meet Your Body Elemental

Take a moment to still your mind before doing the following visualization. You may want to read the questions before starting, or record yourself reading the questions and then play them back, or enlist a friend to read them to you.

Go to a private, quiet place and close your eyes.... You will ask your body elemental some questions and the answers will come easily to you. (Pause to receive answers after each question).

❖ Are your eyes and ears healthy? Is there anything you could do to strengthen them?

❖ Look at your heart and lungs. Are they healthy and is there anything you could do to strengthen them?

❖ Examine each of the following organs individually to see if they are healthy and if there is anything you could do to strengthen them. Your liver, spleen, pancreas, gall bladder, kidneys, adrenals, genital organs and bones.

❖ Ask your body elemental if there is anything it would like you to do differently in your life, such as eating or not eating certain foods, adding or eliminating certain thoughts.

❖ Is there any other question that you would like to ask your body elemental? If so, you will hear, see, or feel the answer now.

❖ Is there anything else your body elemental would like to communicate to you? If so, hear, see, or feel the answer now.

❖ Thank your body elemental for its continual support in all your lifetimes and for speaking with you today. Ask how and where you can contact it again?

Remember all that you learned in this visualization. Take a moment to reflect on your answers before opening your eyes. Record what you learned in your journal.

Beings of the Inner Earth

As our third eye opens and we access the frequencies of the higher mental body, we encounter many unknown beings both inhabitants of this planet and from other stars that want to interact with us. They have been here all along; but we have not seen them. One of the most important are the beings that live in the heart of the Earth.

These beings are descended from Hyperboreans who once lived on the Earth's surface in the second and third cycle of Earth evolution. Their evolution has gone along a different path from humanity and they are developing different gifts. There was antipathy between the two streams of evolution in earlier cycles, so they were separated. As humans become conscious in the fourth and fifth dimensions (which is occurring now), they will become aware of the existence of these beings, and then we will work together for the betterment of other species on the planet.

One account of the inhabitants of the inner Earth is found in the book *Etidorhpa* by John Uri Lloyd, which was first published in 1895. This book describes the journey to the inner Earth of a human visitor who is guided by one of its inhabitants. This book is a true account of an inhabitant of inner Earth, who was chosen as an ambassador to humans to teach us certain principles of science. Inhabitants of the inner Earth have a deeper understanding than humans do of the principles of time, space, and gravity. They are able to use these principles for telepathy, levitation and movement through time and space without machines.

Inhabitants of the inner Earth are great alchemists who work with Gaia (the Earth) directly. They have great knowledge of the mineral kingdom. They are able to move rock with their minds and to encourage minerals to amalgamate with other minerals to make substances not known to humans at this time. These substances have properties that are both harder than what we now know, and softer, even almost to the liquid state. These beings work with crystals, and crystals are their friends. They grow crystals unknown to humans on the Earth's surface. Some of these are on the five unmanifested rays.

Members of this group shared this knowledge with humans during Atlantean times. This facilitated scientific inventions, such as flying machines, building pyramids by lifting blocks of stone telepathically, and using advanced laws of magnetism and gravity. Such knowledge led to the destruction of Atlantis because humans had not overcome their egos in order to build according to divine law. When this destruction occurred, the beings of the inner Earth were horrified and withdrew from humans. Since then, they have had only limited contact with humans who are helping Earth with her evolution.

Presently, the Earth and all beings who live on its surface are moving consciously into the fourth and fifth dimensions. There are certain places on the Earth's surface that are already in those dimensions. Also, there are places on the Earth that are heavier than the third dimension. Individuals from the inner Earth are most likely to be found in the fourth dimension in the Andes of South America, and in the Himalayas of Tibet, India and Nepal. They can exist for only short periods of time in our third dimension as it is too heavy for them.

Some beings of the inner Earth have been monks or lamas in Tibet and in other high mountain ranges. Their skin is very white and their heads are hairless and larger per body size than that of the average human. In their original form their bodies are thin and have less muscle and bone than ours. Their eyes are very different from ours, almost as if they had no eyes. There are legends in Tibet of great lamas who are in a constant state of meditation and who teach with closed eyes. These beings of the inner Earth answer this description.

Just as elementals have entered human evolution, so have some individuals from the inner Earth. An albino is often a hybrid between this race and humans. Some of the same genes, which are recessive in the race from the inner Earth, are recessive in human albinos. The albino is neither one, nor the other, but a mutation of the two. There has been and continues to be a great deal of genetic engineering conducted on various Earth species. Highly evolved beings, who reside in higher dimensions, engage in this genetic engineering between groups of beings. They work according to divine law and are overseen by the equivalent of the Karmic Boards of all groups that are involved.

The electromagnetic field within which humans live is reversed for the inhabitants of the inner Earth. If they desire to do so, inhabitants of the inner Earth are able to reverse their polarities to exist in humanity's fourth dimension. Furthermore, these beings have such advanced knowledge that they are able to reverse the polarity of humans who wish to enter their realm. As we learn to work with our body elemental and to control the etheric, astral and mental dimensions, we will be able to change our polarity to enter the world of the beings of the inner Earth. All those with the incorrect polarity cannot enter. In fact, they would not even be aware of the openings into the Earth if they stood right beside them.

As we begin to master the negative polarity of de-manifestation, we can work with these beings. Humans are usually more skilled working with the positive polarity of manifestation, but learning to balance and to work equally well with both polarities is necessary in order to be a full co-creator. This is alchemy, which has much in common with cooking. To be a good cook, you need to know how much of each ingredient to use to get the best taste. If you are making custard, it will only set if there are the right amounts of milk, egg and sugar cooked at the appropriate temperature. In a similar way, our Creator makes the cosmic stew, which is the universe.

Evolution of Animals

Humans have a tendency to exaggerate their own importance and to forget that animals, reptiles, birds, fish, insects, flowers, trees, and minerals are evolving on our planet as well. We are meant to be guardians of the Earth and its life forms. Because we have been irresponsible, some aspects of this role have been taken from us. However, as we grow into responsibility during the next two thousand years, the care of these other life forms will once again be placed in our hands.

Until the Lemurian cycle, animals were developing on the planet along with other species in accordance with their evolution. These animals were precursors and not identical to what they are today. Laggards tampered with their evolution and created animals as servants and for their own amusement. They altered each species of animal, such as wolves, large cats, elephants, giraffes, deer, bears and monkeys, to have one dominant characteristic.

These qualities are recognized as gifts by many First Nations people of North America, who have adopted an animal as either a personal, or tribal, totem. As such, a person might be a member of the bear or wolf clan, thereby having the protection and specific characteristics of that animal. Likewise, the Chinese acknowledge their connections to animals by appointing different animals for each year. For example, they have the years of the tiger, rat, pig and rabbit. In fact, each human being has a relationship to one animal more than to another, even if we are not aware of this.

Qualities of Some Animals

Lion	Courage
Bull	Sexual prowess/ potency
Elephant	Wisdom
Dog/Wolf	Loyalty
Seal/Otter	Playful
Deer	Innocence/purity
Horse	Speed
Hyena	Ruthlessness
Monkey	Mischievousness
Coyote	Cunning
Cat	Independence

Figure 10 - This list is a starting point for contemplating the qualities of all animals – even those not listed.

After the Laggards isolated specific qualities of animals, they could no longer develop as intended. They were not able to develop an individual ego and continued to evolve as part of a group soul. Therefore, they were not able to develop their unique gifts and abilities. Intrinsic to this process is a level of emotional and mental maturity. Animals do not have this ability to the same extent as humans. However, many animals have rudimentary ability in free will and other qualities that humans value, such as love, knowledge and loyalty. Many species of animals interact and develop a little of the qualities of the other species through this interaction. One of the reasons that human beings resist seeing the intelligence of animals is that it would be difficult to kill and eat them, torture them for science, and eradicate their species if we acknowledged their intelligence. The books *When Elephants Weep* by Jeffrey Moussaleff, *Dogs that know when their owners are coming home* by Rupert Sheldrake, and *Animals in Translation* by Temple Grandin are excellent sources on emotional and mental intelligence in animals.

Some animals have found a way to quicken their individual gifts through association with humans. Many cats, dogs and birds are equivalent to avatars and are wayshowers for their species within animal evolution. Through associating with humans, they become more conscious, and when they die they take that consciousness back to their group soul. This hastens the process of emotional and mental development for their species. Even some wild animals, such as chimpanzee and gorillas, befriend humans.

Some animals that live in zoos are there to remind humans about their responsibility to animals. These individual animals sacrifice their freedom in order to assist the rest of their race. For example, some dolphins in captivity are bodhisattvas who sacrifice themselves on behalf of their race to increase compassion in humans for other sentient life forms. When these animal avatars die, they give what they have learned back to their group soul. However, these few animals cannot raise their species to consciousness by themselves.

To continue their evolution as planned, animals are leaving Earth. This is one of the reasons why species are becoming extinct. Many animals are ready to leave their group soul and to individualize. To do this, they must recover the remainder of their original personality which will happen in the next cycle of their evolution. However, even in the future, these evolved animals will have one particular characteristic that is stronger and more noticeable than another. Animals have been set back millions of years and the Laggards who did this have incurred a penalty. Animals will go to another Eden outside this solar system, for they have earned beauty, peace and a pure beginning.

Some animals even go against the ways of their own species in order to join another. That was true of my family's cat. My folks had a hardware store and Mom had a box of kittens that a woman asked her to give away at Christmas. Mom, always an animal lover said "yes" despite my father's reservations. One kitten remained on December the 25th and Mom decided to bring it home "just until the store re-opened in a few days." My father was dubious but complied, but, "Only for those few days. After all, we've got Heidi (the old dog)," said Dad. Also, we identified ourselves as dog, not cat, lovers in our family.

A temporary name was given and home "Kitty" came. Heidi was not keen especially when Kitty ignored the milk suitable for a kitten and preferred to eat dog food out of Heidi's bowl. Then, when Heidi was asleep Kitty snuggled into her warm fur for a cuddle. Kitty had decided to adopt us, dog and all, and within two days Dad had become her favourite human and, as I'm sure you've guessed, Kitty never did return to the store. Within a few months Kitty was joining Heidi and Dad for their walks, a decision she had made without a lead, and had become as close to a dog as a cat is likely to get.

Exercise 19: Your Power Animals

Take a moment to still your mind before answering the following questions in your journal.

Often we are attracted to one animal more than another. We identify the strengths of that animal as ours.

❖ Close your eyes and visualize, or hear, the name of an animal. Write the name of that animal. Repeat this process three times until you have the name of three animals.

❖ Often the first animal you saw is the image that you project to others. What is that image? What qualities from this animal do you project to others?

❖ Often the second animal is the way that others see you. What is that image? What qualities from this animal do others see in you?

❖ Often the third animal is the way we really are. What is that image? What qualities from this animal do you have?

❖ What animal would you avoid being? Why? What observations can you make about yourself because of this?

Evolution of Reptiles and Birds

Reptiles were brought to the Earth semi-formed and neither Laggards nor humanity has tampered with their evolution. Reptiles, such as snakes, lizards and tortoise, are cold-blooded and from a cold planet where they cared only for themselves. Some, like the dinosaurs, were instinctual and greedy for self. They were brought to Earth to develop warmth and concern for others. Most reptiles, like the dinosaurs, did not do this and became extinct here.

One of the last remnants of the dinosaurs, the Tuatara of Tasmania, has found a unique way to learn to love. It shares a burrow with the Mutton-bird. When the Mutton-bird lays its first egg, the Tuatara eats it. However, it looks after all the other eggs. It cleans the nest, keeps the nestlings clean, and guards them when the parents are away. Through this, the Tuatara has learned to co-operate, trust, and care for another species.

To survive, some reptiles made themselves smaller, soaked up the sun of their environment and evolved. Some snakes, such as garters, desired to be warm-blooded and have learned to birth their young live rather than lay eggs. The Earth is a planet of love and it teaches its inhabitants to develop the principle of compassion. Because of this, reptiles, which are unable to develop concern for others, will die out on Earth, whereas reptiles that develop these qualities will continue their evolution.

Science has recently discovered that birds are descended from reptiles. Birds were cold-blooded reptiles that through caring for others became warm-blooded. Birds and dinosaurs came from different planets in the same solar system in another galaxy than ours. The bird race was placed on Earth to evolve with humanity. They, like humanity, were seedlings, and the ones who oversee our evolution thought that the two races would be compatible. Bird evolution, unlike animal and human evolution, has not been tampered with by the Laggards or humanity. Birds came to Earth in the first cycle of human evolution when the planet was still misty. Birds kept their light form because they did not want to be trapped in the heavier earth element.

Myths relate many stories of our relationship with birds. The West Coast North American indigenous people, the Haida, say the Raven helped to create the Earth and it tricks humanity into evolving. The

Haida have only two totems for their tribe, Raven and Eagle. These birds are still important today and a person is a member of either the Raven or the Eagle clan and marriage between members of the same clan is discouraged.

Many Native Americans also speak of the thunderbird, the messenger between the Creator and humanity. We might think these thunderbirds are creatures only of our imagination but some myths, as we have come to know, are based on reality. American farmers in the central states have occasionally seen thunderbirds and describe them as gigantic birds that emerge as if out of the Void prior to violent thunderstorms. Thunderbirds are able to appear at that time because of the change in electrical polarities between the dimensions where they exist and our third dimension. Larry Arnold, author of *Ablaze: The mysterious fires of spontaneous human combustion*, one of the world's leading experts on spontaneous combustion, has been gathering evidence on thunderbirds for years.

Acknowledging the intelligence of birds will totally change the way we treat them. For example, humans are not the only toolmaker on the planet, as birds are known to make tools to attract mates, build nests, and obtain food. Parrots have the intelligence of at least a two-year-old child and can be toilet trained, count, carry on sophisticated conversation, and, sadly, even become mentally ill when mistreated.

In the future there will be many professions that study other species to learn both their specific gifts and also interspecies communication. Jane Goodall, in her work with chimpanzees, and Dian Fossey, in her work with gorillas, were forerunners in this important area of study. Also, animal psychologists and whisperers, to name a few professions, are teaching us how to co-evolve responsibly with other species.

In many ways, birds have vastly superior sensing functions to those of humans. Birds' sight is far better than ours, and they see greater distances and in greater detail. They see all colours that we see as well as colours that are invisible to us. With their acute feeling and sensing they can feel the breeze change before it happens. They sense the time of the day, know the type of weather before it arrives and also sense immanent danger. Their feathers actually act as a kind of antenna to pick up this kind of information. Scientists may call this sense instinct as a way of negating its importance, but it is a kind of intuition. Birds are able to teach humans to improve their sensing function and, if we attempt to perceive the world as a bird does, we will develop these characteristics.

Birds are able to move through the Void, and many species of birds travel in the fourth dimension. Co-development, co-existence and co-support between bird and humanity are essential. We have always been in awe of the bird's ability to fly, and we can learn to levitate and move in the air. Many well-documented examples of people levitating prove that it is possible. Also, we will develop the ability to project our essence to various parts of the world and to rematerialize our physical body. Understanding bird evolution and their ability to move into the fourth dimension will help us to learn some of the many ways this can be accomplished.

In Lemuria some bird species, which decided to live on the sea, acquired webbed feet. At that time, birds were already a range of colours and sizes but they were less visible, less solid, and more like gusts of air than birds of the present day. Birds are evolving a body that is able to fly and still be solid. Just as we can learn from birds, so they can learn from us. Humans teach birds to evolve in the third dimensional physical realm. Overall, both races are evolving at equal speeds.

One of the reasons that birds have been placed on Earth is that there are great beings, which look like birds and are kin to them, who are helping both bird and humanity develop. One of these is the Egyptian God Horus, the son of Isis and Osiris, who was portrayed as a great hawk although his parents wore human bodies. These beings are involved with genetic programming of human-bird hybrids evolving on this planet and more is said about them in the chapter *Sirius, The Cosmic Dragon and The Pleiades* on page 160.

I have a soft spot for birds of the parrot family and have shared my home with parakeets, cockatoos and lastly a lovebird by the name of Lucie. All have been free to fly in the house and they became as close family members as the cats and dogs. Lucie was a bodhisattva bird and much in advance of most lovebirds. To give you an idea about her extraordinary personality, I'd like to share her story with you.

On Santa Lucia's day, sprawled on a heating pad in a shoebox, the baby lovebird arrived. "Could you look after her for the weekend?" asked my exhausted friend, handing her over. Falling out of the nest, abandoned by parents, needing to be fed every four hours, the little preemie was doomed to extinction. No time for one when you raise hundreds. Setting the alarm clock, I committed to motherhood, all weekend carrying the naked nestling under my sweater close to my heart. By Monday I'd fallen in love.

As feathers sprouted, her outings began up the bra strap and out the neck, staring curiously at the new world before descending again for comfort. Longer forays to the shoulder, loving nibbles on neck and ears, fascinated by earrings, mine and everyone else's. Lucie loved all visitors, claiming humans as hers. Playing hide and seek behind dishes, rolling marbles across the floor, chewing ends off shoelaces, happily entertaining herself…for a while. I, working two floors up hear her call, "Ca Ha, Ca Ha?" This, translated into lovebird lingo, means, "Where are you?" I wait. A few minutes later, having hopped up the stairs of Everest, Lucie, the conquering hero, waddles through the doorway, and ascends the pant leg onto my shoulder.

Exercise 20: Your Relationship with Birds and Reptiles

Take a moment to still your mind before answering the following questions in your journal.

❖ Which bird do you favour? Imagine that you are that bird. What qualities do you have? How can you practice those qualities in your life?

❖ Which bird are you least attracted to? Imagine you are that bird. What qualities do you have? Do you or others have some of those qualities? How can you learn appreciation and respect for these qualities?

❖ Do you feel an affinity for any member of the reptile family? If so, which one?

❖ Imagine that you are a member of the reptile family. Which kind? What qualities do you have? How could these be helpful in your life?

Fish and Water Species

Fish were put on this planet to enjoy the waters and to be a source of beauty for humanity. They are the jewels of the water, just as semiprecious stones are the jewels of the earth. Fish, like minerals, come in all the colours that are found on the twelve rays that make up creation. Humans are only now beginning to see some colours and others will become visible in the future. When the Greek poet Homer wrote *The Odyssey* over two thousand years ago, he spoke of the ocean as wine coloured because humans at that time were not able to differentiate the many colours of blue. Even now some people have difficulty differentiating green and red and are said to be colour blind.

A coral reef is the best place to view all the colours in the sea. Unfortunately, it is becoming increasingly difficult to experience this as we are killing off reefs at an alarming rate. Coral gardens can exist only within a few degrees of temperature and the heating of our oceans is eradicating them.

Earth is a water planet attuned to the emotional body of all species that live here. Because water is a conductor both of positive and negative frequencies, humans will not be able to stabilize emotions or clear their negativity until they clean up their waters, both inside and outside.

Whales, dolphins and fish are dying from an accumulation of toxins and garbage like plastics, which humans have dumped into the ocean. We have over-fished and need to eliminate dragnets to allow fish to recover. We need to nurture and keep diversity in species. Fish farms cannot replace healthy wild fish any more than a person living in prison will be as healthy as one able to breathe the fresh air and feel the sun's rays on his face.

Our negative involvement with water species is far from recent. Fish were originally not predatory, but in Atlantis we tampered with their evolution and created predators, such as sharks, for our amusement. These predators feed off the negativity that we create in the water through the violence that takes place there. There are two keys to motivate us to assist the earth, water and air species. The first is self-interest, that is to say, if we don't clean up these habitats, there will no longer be humans. The second key is to activate our conscience through understanding how truly intelligent these various species are.

Let's examine the intelligence of a water dweller that bears no physical resemblance to humans, unlike the dolphin we spoke of earlier. I'm speaking of the octopus. The octopus has the intelligence of at least a two-year-old human child. It might be much more than that, but unfortunately, we view intelligence based on how well other species can perform tasks in human-like fashion. This is a kind of racial prejudice.

In an experiment to test intelligence, scientists put an octopus in one tank and its favourite food, crab, in another. The octopus was given various skill-testing tasks and was rewarded with a crab. The octopus was doing well on these tests when something completely unexpected occurred. The scientists noticed that the number of crabs decreased nightly. They decided to turn the lights down low in order to simulate night time conditions and to watch from behind a blind to see what happened. They witnessed the octopus climb out of its tank, crawl down the table leg onto the floor. From there it crawled up the legs of the table on which the crabs were kept and into the aquarium with the crabs. You can imagine what happened next. The octopus enjoyed a tasty meal and then crawled back the way it had come to its own container. It makes one wonder how the intelligence of the octopus and other water inhabitants would be assessed if we could see them without our human preconceptions.

Insects

While the animals, reptiles, fish and birds all were meant to evolve on this planet, insects have a different history. When the Laggards came to Earth, their strong thoughts of irritation, anger, frustration and resentment eventually took form as insects. In most cases, this was not deliberate, but rather a by-product of negative thoughts that coalesced over time into physical forms. As we transmute our negative thoughts, the annoying insect species will disappear. Killing insects with chemicals is like putting a bandage on a cancerous growth rather than uprooting it, and this behaviour results not in fewer insects, but more.

Insects are wonderful teaching tyrants for us. Buddhists recommend that we refrain from killing insects, and by doing so, we learn from them. Insects give us opportunities to overcome our own irritation, resentment, and many of the other negative feelings that they stir up in us. Ants, for example, are reminders to us of our own self-importance. Ants are industrious, working to make their colonies grow and even raising other insects, such as aphids, for food. Ants have roles and work together, but they do not benefit other species. Isn't this sometimes true of humanity?

Insects are a kingdom unto themselves. Bees, ants, termites, wasps and hornets all have a group soul and yet, within the group soul, each individual has a specific purpose. The three major roles for such insects are as queens meant to lay eggs, as drones meant to fertilize queens, and as workers meant to keep the hive alive. In addition to these roles, some insects, like humanity, have warrior classes that protect the nest.

In insects, the instinct for group preservation is higher than that for individual preservation. In a bee colony, many queens are grown to maturity but only the strongest survives by stinging the other queens to death. The others forfeit their lives for the good of the whole. Scientists mistakenly call this behaviour instinct, but it is really the bees listening to the divine plan. Bees, ants and termites are able to evolve as a species having only a group soul, and no individualization, but they will never become co-creators. As individualization is only one evolutionary path, it is detrimental for us to exaggerate its importance.

All insects exist in the constant now where there is no past, present, or future. Insects are in balance with being, which is the feminine, or yin, principal. The few male insects have a very limited role of fertilization. The majority of insects are neutered females who become fertile when they are given hormones.

Bees are one species of insects that have benefited humanity greatly. Bees are minor versions of an intelligent race that is native to Venus and are one of the earlier attempts to integrate Venutian life on Earth. The bee does not have a stinger on Venus, but on Earth the bee is a hybrid that defends itself against threats. It produces honey, which is sustenance for humanity and other species. It is potentially dangerous as some individuals are allergic to the venom and yet the venom is also a remedy for arthritis. A bee hums and vibrates on its soul level. Perhaps we would be more in keeping with the divine plan if we did likewise. A bee understands its relationship to all members of its group soul. It is a part of them, and they are a part of it.

How Insects Resemble Humans

Insects	Part of our personality
Mosquito/ Tick	Draws blood from others
Fly	Annoys others
Hornet	Aggressive to others
Termite	Undermines others' foundations
Bee	Sacrifices itself to benefit others
Ant	Industrious & determined
Praying Mantis	Hypocritical, devious
Cockroach	Going where we are not wanted
Cricket/Cicada	Pleasant song
Lady Bug/ Beetle	Armoured
Butterfly	Transformation

Figure 11 - This list is the starting point for contemplating all insects – even those not listed.

The butterfly is another beneficial insect. Butterflies epitomize the inevitability of our path to consciousness. Not only are there thousands of species of butterflies, but each one is unique just as each one of us is totally unique, and our process of transformation leads to the same final result. There are four cycles that the butterfly undergoes in its transformation from egg, to caterpillar, to cocoon before finding its final grace and beauty as a butterfly. These are stages that humans also undergo in our journey from unconsciousness, dominated by the personality, to conscious partnership with the soul.

In the egg—the first stage of transformation—individuals are unconscious. Obedient and never questioning the rules, they are at the mercy of their environment. Because they are passive, others control them, and their careers are usually unplanned. These unconscious individuals buy the lottery ticket of life and hope that they will win the big payoff, through luck but no effort to become conscious. Men and women in the egg stage do not consciously harm others or their environment, nor do they consciously improve it.

The second stage of transformation is that of the caterpillar. Our world and organizations have been run by caterpillars whose insatiable appetite to have more has destroyed their environment. People in the caterpillar stage of transformation step over others in their path in order to reach their ego-centered goals. They are greedy to have the best that money can buy and have little conscience as to how the needs of others are met. I am not suggesting malevolence, just a "me-first" attitude. Natural resources exist only to meet the needs of the caterpillar. Individuals in this stage do not act as if they care how many trees they cut down, minerals they extract, or air they pollute. While the egg is passive and dependent, the caterpillar is aggressive and independent. Although it still cannot create new life, the caterpillar is further along the path of transformation than the egg because it makes choices. It chooses which plants to eat and can move to an environment more suitable to its preferences.

Cocooning, the third stage in transformation, is a time of rest and emptiness. Cocooning refers to people who withdraw from the world and prefer to stay home and enjoy simple pleasures. Men and women might cocoon by leaving their highly paid, stressful jobs with large organizations to work at home for themselves or for a lower-paid job with less responsibility. This also happens when an individual takes a sabbatical to meditate and reflect on the purpose of life, or moves to the country for a more peaceful environment. Cocooning is an inner time when you ask yourself how you can make a difference to others and the Earth and when you let go of the status and roles that have kept you attached to the material world. On the surface it doesn't appear as if much is happening, but inside the cocoon the transformation from caterpillar to butterfly is occurring.

At this time in our human evolution many men and women are going through this cocoon stage. They know that being an egg or a caterpillar are no longer options. They have the desire to become a butterfly and so withdraw from their previous ways of being to reflect and meditate. These individuals are creating a space to allow the universe to complete their process of transformation. By surrender to the process of divine will our transformation naturally takes place and we become the unique individual that we really are.

Butterflies are the last stage in the process of transformation. Men and women in their butterfly stage are free of both their culture's rules and their personality's drives. Formerly, they were found more often on the fringes of society, living alternative lifestyles. Often they were the craftspeople, artists, writers, environmentalists, social activists, healers, spiritual teachers and others who brought beauty, love and wisdom into the world. Formerly, there were fewer butterflies in the traditional workforce, but this is changing now.

Because of the economic downturn, increased violence and threat of war, along with increased environmental disasters, individuals in all walks of life are seriously questioning the old paradigm of unlimited growth and more for "me" on which the bulk of our organizations have been based. The organizational caterpillar is dying and many people are well into the cocoon stage looking for a new way of being and doing in the world. The new way is that of the butterfly.

Feeding on nectar and water, butterflies are creatures of beauty who destroy nothing in their path. Butterflies are also the breeders—the fertile ones who create the eggs to ensure the continuance of their race. But they do more than this. They fly from flower to flower pollinating them, thereby assuring the continuance of other species in the world. Butterflies are beings of air and soul, not bound, like caterpillars, to the earth. They are delicate and easily damaged by an unfriendly environment. But they are also tenacious and—as with monarchs—able to fly thousands of miles to find the right environment to create new life.

Butterflies are soul-infused women and men who assist others on their paths to consciousness. They are fertile and creative and being around them catalyzes new growth in both others and their organizations. As we enter the fourth (butterfly) cycle of human evolution, these soul-infused individuals are the forerunners and the wayshowers of the principles of interdependence. They are the pioneers who will help to birth the new paradigm of co-creation in our organizations, in our relationships and in our world. The butterfly has been the symbol of our International Institute for Transformation since its inception in 2000 and it was the symbol for my personal corporation for the two decades preceding this. I choose the butterfly for two reasons. It has been a symbol for the soul since the time of the ancient Greek culture and my life is dedicated to helping individuals to become soul-infused personalities. Also, the butterfly is a symbol of generous gifting to other species on the Earth, for creating beauty wherever it goes and for incredible strength and endurance in a seemingly fragile frame. These qualities touch my heart deeply and I believe many, many others are touched as well. These are noble qualities to strive for in our life and work and, as we enter the Aquarian Age, to hold in our hearts during the difficult transition when the caterpillar of our collective humanity dies and we exit from its cocoon.

Exercise 21: Four Stages of Your Life

Take a moment to still your mind before answering the following questions in your journal.

❖ Examine your life as if you were a butterfly.

❖ What did you learn in the egg stage and when did you leave it? Did something occur to move you to the next stage?

❖ What did you learn in the caterpillar stage and when did you leave it? Did something occur to move you to the next stage?

❖ What did you learn in the cocoon stage and when did you leave it? Did something occur to move you to the next stage?

❖ What helped you to transform into a butterfly?

❖ Are there aspects of the other three stages that you still cling to? If so, what do you need to leave these stages behind?

Plants

Everything is alive. This is one of the most important tenets to uphold if we are to become conscious co-creators. To know this in theory is the first step, then to actually experience it in daily life is the next step. What separates animate from what we choose to call inanimate is consciousness and the ability to evolve. This means that rocks, sand, and plants are animate, and a table or a rug, even though it is composed of atoms that are alive, is inanimate. Because angels and elementals are often depicted with eyes, ears and look relatively human it is easier, for many people, to view them as conscious whereas it is more difficult to believe this of stones and plants. In such an anthropomorphic view of the world, only what looks like us is seen as alive, and needing to be protected and cherished.

However, in the last several decades, there has been progress in altering this perception. In the book, *The Secret Life of Plants,* author Peter Tompkins reviews scientific evidence illustrating that plants thrive when we send positive thoughts their way and wither when we send negative thoughts. Plants, in fact, are more highly evolved in their stream of evolution than humans are in theirs. This is a humbling thought. And why is this? Plants live in harmony with divine law and serve others, which is the highest law of life. They create oxygen so we are able to breathe. They are beautiful and colourful so we experience joy. They give their bodies to us as food and as wood to build houses and furniture for our shelter and comfort.

Humans have tampered genetically with the evolution of the plant kingdom more than with any other kingdom. In most cases, we don't foresee the long-range impact of what we do. We are erasing the diversity of species by attempting to create plants that produce more. We cut down old growth forests and replace them with two or three species of trees. We plant only one kind of wheat and create fruit with no seeds, or genetically modified tomatoes with thick skins that pack better. We kill the goodness of food at an atomic level by radiation and ingest dead matter when we eat it. Eating radiated and genetically modified food are two of the unhealthiest things that we are currently doing to our bodies. This short-range thinking weakens the complex web of life within which we all live.

What we call weeds are undesirable plants and many of these

have been created by genetic tampering by humans. Some weeds, like poison ivy, are destructive and others, such as stinging nettle, have both negative and positive functions. Nettle causes pain if exposed to skin and yet, makes an excellent blood purifier and is a tasty food to eat.

If we closely examine the plant kingdom, we observe that plants perform a service for the Earth and live in harmony with it. All species have a special function on this planet. Members of the plant kingdom, which include trees, vegetables, grains, flowers, moss on the land and in the water algae, seaweed, and so on, are givers. Plants give to us in many ways. Some heat us; others cool us. The desert cactus provides water and fruit to the traveller and has adapted its service to its surroundings. Some provide gateways to other dimensions, whether these are grapes for wine, or mushrooms and cactus for creating altered states. The scents of some plants, such as the rose, lilac and lavender, heal various maladies. Many medicinals—the healers of the plant kingdom—are being wiped out at an alarming rate in jungles that we destroy to create farmland. We are doing this before we even know their value. Even the roots of some plants are eaten and all roots anchor moisture in the soil and break down minerals to create soil for new life.

Plants evolve as a group soul and some are more highly evolved than others. Old trees, for example, have elementals called *devas* with their own personalities. The Druids spoke of sacred trees among which they categorized the oak, yew, hawthorn and holly. In acknowledging their sacredness, the Druids acknowledged their evolved consciousness.

Plants have more energy when they are native to their environment. Therefore, it is more energizing for us to eat food that is grown where we live. Also, it is preferable to eat plants in their season. If we live in cold climates, it is preferable to eat root vegetables in the winter than to eat lettuce. Even animals know this. Have you noticed dogs and cats eating grass in the spring? Grass acts as a tonic and cleanser and animals sense this intuitively and are drawn to it for their health.

It is also easier on our bodies to eat the food of our genetic history. So if we come from Irish stock, it is easier on our body to eat potatoes than rice. It takes several generations for the body to change from that of a meat eater to that of a vegetarian. As well as our physical genetic history, however, we also need to take into account our spiritual history. So if the eating of meat repulses us and our body does not need it for health, then it is good to honour our intuition. All of us are different in what we need to eat in order to be healthy. In the seventh cycle of human evolution, which we are now entering, self-sustaining agriculture will be essential.

My passion for learning more about plants has increased over the years. They say that it takes seven years to make a garden and that is true based on my experience. The first year in my present home I watched the existing garden that the previous owners had for forty years to see what lived there already. The second year I became a massive pruner and the third a diligent weeder, although in retrospect I should have reversed that order. Only in the fourth year was I ready to move plants, to take out some and put in others. In the fifth year I learned how to prune fruit trees and started growing many different kinds. Now in the sixth year I am finally ready to learn about vegetable gardening. Each year gets easier and more beauty appears so I eagerly wait to see what will happen this seventh year.

My attitude to weeds has also altered over these last six years. In the early years I attempted to keep the lawn weed-free and did not succeed. Now my attitude to "weeds" has altered. I have become friends with dandelions and all sorts of "weeds" that have beautiful flowers in the lawn. My garden has been one of my greatest teachers in listening to the voice of Mother Earth.

Exercise 22: Plants and You

Take a moment to still your mind before answering the following questions in your journal.

- ❖ What plants, such as vegetables and fruit, do you feel healthiest eating? How often do you eat them?
- ❖ What plants, or other foods, do you feel least healthy eating? How often do you eat them?
- ❖ Name the flower you most drawn to? Its colour, season for blooming, texture, scent. What do you feel is its purpose?
- ❖ What tree are you most drawn to? What is its purpose?

Properties of Minerals and Gemstones

Just as we require vitamins from plants to keep us alive, we need minerals from the earth. Minerals are the heaviest elements found on Earth. Minerals are evolving even as humans are, but because their frequency is so slow, we tend to think of them as inanimate. This misconception stems from the fact that humans, who along with animals and plants are made up of carbon-based atoms, have come to believe that only carbon-based forms are animate or alive. Carbon forms endless chains and it reacts with anything nearby. We associate this property with life. However, silicon, which is directly below carbon in frequency, does this as well.

Silicon is a form of crystal and the Earth's crust, which is 30 to 50 miles (48 to 80 kilometres) thick, is made up of 87 percent silicon compounds. We are living on a planet made of crystal. This crystal receives energy from the Sun, stores it and gives it to living creatures in the form they need. There are at least a hundred thousand kinds of crystals, built in only six shapes, all of which are derived from the shape of a cube. Similarly, each atomic element has a crystalline structure that also can be reduced to a cube.

Computer chips are made of silicon and televisions, cell phones, and electronics of various kinds rely heavily on silicon-based forms. Even biochips implanted in humans are grown on computers, and artificial intelligence is increasing daily. A time might come, and not in the distant future, when computerized silicon-based forms are recognized as living life forms.

The most highly evolved crystals are gems and semiprecious stones. Gems are the repository in the mineral kingdom of the various rays of which our bodies and everything is composed. Gems and semiprecious stones have been employed throughout human evolution for beauty and in healing. Depending on the stone, they can be ground into an elixir and drunk, placed on a particular chakra or organ, or worn in the form of jewellery to give ongoing energy. In India, Ayurvedic medicine has employed gemstones to heal the physical, emotional, and mental bodies for hundreds, even thousands of years.

In the Ayurvedic system there are three universal forces based on cosmic laws that are continually creating, preserving and destroying both in our inner and outer worlds. This is referred to as the *Tridosha laws*. These forces are present in gems and can be used to alleviate suffering. The positive creative forces are known as *kapha* and are based on the integrating element of water. The negative or destroying force is called *pitta* and is based on the element of fire. The neutral force is *vata*, based on air, and it mixes readily with both pitta and kapha to either preserve or destroy. These three forces are called the three *doshas* and represent the cosmic forces of harmony-vata, energy-pitta, and inertia-kapha. These forces are in every cell in the human body. The stones used mostly for restoring the body to health in Ayurveda are as follows. Ruby and coral are pitta and negative, pearl, diamond and emerald are kapha and positive, topaz and sapphire are vata and neutral.

Hindu astrology also uses gemstones for restoring balance in the bodies, and the colours are important in healing. An individual who has a weak Sun in their astrological chart, for example, might be prone to anaemia. In such a case, ruby, which is red and carries the Sun's energy, is prescribed. A weak Moon, when aspected by Saturn, can produce insanity, so pearls, which are in reality orange and not white in colour, are used. A weak Mars can create piles, and coral can treat this, as it is yellow in essence. When Mercury is weak, boils and ulcers may result. These disorders can be treated by emeralds, which have a green colour. A weak Jupiter may cause vomiting and obesity. These problems can be treated by topaz, which emits blue rays of energy. A weak Venus produces both diabetes and sterility. These can be treated by diamond, which is an indigo colour. Saturn, when weak, can create numerous chronic diseases such as cancer, arthritis, rheumatism, and diseases of the mind, such as foolishness. These diseases may be treated with sapphire, which is a violet colour.

In Hindu astrology, there are two other invisible planets called Rahu and Ketu. Rahu works with ultra-violet, cosmic radiation. A lack of the ultra-violet might lead to people having suicidal tendencies and diseases of the brain and glands. The onyx can help these problems. Ketu works with the infrared cosmic ray and is represented by tiger-eye, which can be employed for boils, skin problems, itching, cancer and asthma.

Most people wear gemstones for beauty and do not consider how the properties of the stones affect their bodies. Minerals can be understood as condensed potent homeopathic amounts of the seven rays of cosmic energy, whose colours we can see in rainbows. In metaphysical terms these are called initiation stones. Some gemstones have a strong effect on our frequency and it is best not to wear these unless our frequency is the same. It is dangerous to continually wear initiation stones prior to mastering the frequencies of those levels, as we have not learned to control the energy and ray that they represent. As initiation stones the ruby may be worn after stabilizing the lower mental body, the sapphire the higher mental, and the diamond after completing the ascension.

Ayurveda and Hindu astrology are just one system in which gems are used and I have only given a brief overview. There are many systems and colours associated with various gemstones, chakras and rays.

Healing stones, on the other hand, are not worn, but are applied externally to specific areas of the body for short periods of time, or they are pulverized and taken internally as an elixir. When you view stones in this light, it might be easier to understand the importance of making conscious choices about which ones to wear as jewellery.

Ruby, like garnet, which also carries the red frequency, is a bloodstone. For healing purposes, ruby might be used by lethargic individuals to energize them. It also pushes people who have a tendency to draw back and be indecisive. It is a restorative and a tonic for the heart and can prolong life. As an initiation stone the ruby might be worn continually by someone who is no longer controlled by the ego. This occurs when we have mastered the energies of the solar plexus.

Sapphire reflects the violet ray. There are star sapphires that have the mark of the cross on them so that the stone looks like a cross on top of a globe. This symbol is the insignia of royalty—the royal purple—and the sapphire has long been considered a royal stone, as kings were supposed to do the Creator's will on Earth by combining temporal with spiritual law.

Sapphire is a very hard stone. Its energy cuts through lies and untruths, and therefore is useful for healing whenever we need clear intent and purpose. This stone has a discerning quality as well as qualities of peace, calm, and coolness. Whereas the ruby heats us up to act, the sapphire cools down the passions and stabilizes the emotions while at the same time giving us a mission and purpose. The sapphire is like an eye standing in one place that is able to see and know all four directions. A sapphire will increase our flexibility so that we are able to examine all points of view and opinions.

Diamond has qualities not unlike sapphire, as it also anchors the Creator's will on Earth. Diamonds work on the indigo ray as do a few, very special, amethysts. The difference between the properties of the diamond and sapphire is that the sapphire works on the emotional and, to some extent, the mental bodies whereas the diamond works on both the mental and physical bodies. The diamond represents the compression that the Creator's thoughts undergo in order to manifest in these lower dimensions. Geologists teach us that diamonds started as coal and became diamonds over millions of years of pressure. Likewise, pressure, force and time are needed to create our spiritual body—which Buddhists call the diamond body, which is made up of our physical, etheric, emotional, lower and higher mental bodies.

Because the diamond comes from coal, it is able to work in the physical as well as the mental world. Ideally, the diamond indicates the complete non-attachment of love in the higher mental body, the diamond body. It is a perfect stone that reflects all rays. It is best not to wear a diamond until we acquire a diamond body, when the five bodies of the personality blend together and reflect all rays. Diamonds, the hardest stones known to humanity, are used as precise cutting tools to cut through less evolved minerals. Likewise, a Master with a diamond body has the ability to cut through the lower planes of existence to help younger brothers and sisters to return to the divine plan.

It is unfortunate that so many people have chosen to wear diamonds as a symbol of their love for another person. Through the power of these stones they are attaching themselves to others in bonded umbilical relationships. This delays their spiritual progress in learning unconditional love, which does not occur until the fourth level of spiritual consciousness. Generally, diamonds are not recommended for healing, as they are such powerful stones. They have far-ranging consequences because they work on all rays. However, if one has a well-developed mental body, the diamond is very useful in cleaning up the remaining effluvia and mental thoughts that lead to incorrect thoughtforms. Only then are diamonds useful for healing purposes.

Properties of Gemstones and Metals

Gemstone	Use
Ruby	Energizes and cures lethargy
Sapphire	Cuts through untruths, stabilizes emotions
Diamond	Reflects all rays and is too powerful for most people
Aquamarine	Allows expression of hurt, sorrow and grief
Turquoise	Opens heart, anus, bowels
Coral	Heals blood diseases
Pearl	Useful to get people in touch with emotions if they are too mental
Moonstone	Opens the subconscious
Lapis	Useful to enter other dimensions the Void
Topaz	Useful to open sexual centers and throat
Amber	Good for women's sexual centers and femininity
Emerald	Good for heart, reinvigoration of the body and depression
Opal	Enhances ability to see the astral realm
Tourmaline	Breaks up both positive and negative karmic patterns. Opens solar plexus Dangerous for pregnant women, those with heart or nerve problems
Onyx	Works on infrared frequency. Helps brain and with suicidal tendencies
Tiger Eye	Works with ultra-violet. Good for boils, skin, asthma, cancer
Gold	Transmutes negative to positive energy and draws poison out of the body. Energy of the Sun
Silver	Works with unconscious energy of the Moon
Copper	Poor man's gold. Helps arthritis, liver, spleen

Figure 12 - Summary of uses for gemstones and precious metals.

Aquamarine can be worn by someone who has mastered the emotional element. If worn continually before then, the aquamarine might capsize the wearer in emotions. For healing purposes, however, the aquamarine is very effective in opening tear ducts and allowing us to express feelings of hurt, pain, sorrow, and grief.

Turquoise is a symbolic stone for those individuals who have mastered the physical body. The turquoise is long revered by Native Americans, especially those of Mexico and Arizona. For healing, turquoise is useful to open the heart and bowels. There are few downsides to wearing turquoise in that most of us in the western world could also use more heart and bowel opening.

Both black and red coral affect the emotional body. Coral is red, which is normally the fire of the third chakra, while at the same time, as it is found in water, it is associated with the second chakra. This combination is needed to heal the blood, which is both fire and water. Ground coral can be added to food to re-establish balance in bladder, kidneys, blood, and any areas in the body that are affected by liquid. Black coral, which is many times the strength of red coral, is employed in severe cases of hepatitis to heal the blood very quickly. However, for gradual healing, red coral is better to stabilize the body after we accomplish the desired effect. Both colours may be employed in the treatment of obesity, lethargy, slovenliness and purposelessness. Coral's healing properties far outweigh any dangers in its use. Wearing coral reminds us that we are both fire and water beings.

Pearl, like coral, is good to purify the blood. It is the diamond of the lower body for, like the diamond, the pearl has the ability to reflect all colours of the rays. But, unlike the diamond, the pearl has not internalized these. All rays affect the pearl so it is not good for an emotional individual to wear. It is useful, however, for someone who is very mental and who is not expressing his or her feelings. Pearls are helpful in strengthening the second chakra. It is preferable to employ white and pink pearls to help people open up rather than grey and black pearls, for these would lead the person to express more negativity. A perfect pearl is better for this purpose than a deformed one. Deformed pearls, although not stable, have the ability to see all points of view in the water element. Unfortunately, they have not acquired the ability to hold a perfect shape when they are bombarded with feelings, which is an important quality.

The moonstone's gift is in working with the unmanifested world. Whereas aquamarine and pearl work with the light side of the emotional element of the body, moonstone works with the dark, subconscious forces of the emotional element. The black diamond is also able to unlock the door to the powerful darker elements of the subconscious, but the moonstone is preferable.

Lapis lazuli can take us into the Void, the etheric space that lies behind our manifested world. Lapis lazuli is commonly bluish or indigo in colour and it is useful to open the third eye chakra to enter other dimensions.

Topaz helps to open both the throat and most especially the sexual centres. Topaz brings the Sun down to the Earth, the mental down to the physical. Topaz establishes a link between the solar plexus and the root chakra. Topaz assists any organs below the navel, such as female and male organs and lower intestines. This stone also might be employed to join the energy from the sexual organs to the throat where it is used to heal tonsils, vocal cords and tongue. It is also good for rest and nerve strength. Because its chemical composition is similar to sapphire, it is sometimes referred to as the yellow sapphire. Like sapphire, topaz works with the vata, the air element, and has a neutral energy in the body. Someone who has stabilized his or her emotions might wear the topaz continually.

Amber has many of the same properties as topaz and has no negative effects if worn continually. Not really a mineral, amber is actually petrified tree resin, but it can be used as if it were a mineral stone. Amber is especially helpful with women's sexual organs and is respected by many tribal people including Bedouin and Tibetans.

Emerald is a very stable stone that is helpful in opening and stabilizing the heart centre and the growth of the entire body. Emerald is good for general cleansing, reinvigoration, and relieving exhaustion. It cleanses the blood and liver, renews cell growth and clears fog around the brain. Emeralds, like quartz crystals, are affectionate stones, which become quite attached to their wearers.

Opal is both a water and fire stone. There is so much water in it that it is counterproductive in stabilizing the emotional body. Psychics, or those who wish to develop that quality, might wish to use opals to enhance their ability to see in the astral realm, but only if they are emotionally stable themselves. Ancient Persians thought of the opal as a sacred stone because of its quality of fire on water.

Tourmaline brings forth the same energy that was invoked by the Incas and Aztecs when they sacrificed one individual for the good of all. Jesus' communion of the last supper served the same purpose when he says, "This is my blood of the New Testament which is shed for many for the remission of sins." Thus, sometimes, we might find it painful to work with tourmaline. Then why bother?

Tourmaline is one of the most powerful gems to break up both positive and negative karmic patterns. It helps to bring these patterns consciously to our attention so that we might choose what to keep and what to eliminate. Tourmaline is a fibrous stone, which is like an umbilical cord that connects the physical and emotional bodies. It does not work very much with the mental body, but it has a very potent effect on the etheric body. Tourmaline opens the solar plexus and, initially, it is preferable to apply it to that area for no more than five to ten minutes a day so that the area will not become raw. We must work cautiously with tourmaline. It might be dangerous for pregnant women, or for those who have heart or nerve problems, as it has a tenacious ability to penetrate and move.

Onyx has a very high frequency, which is on the ultra-violet—the coldest cosmic ray. It can be used for excessive heat complaints, hyperactivity, insomnia and excessive vata-air problems. Conversely, tiger-eye is anchored to the Earth and works on the infrared—the hottest cosmic ray. This low frequency is good for healing bone. Tiger-eye strengthens cartilage and the backbone that must be strong to conduct the kundalini energy. It is also good for paralysis and to remove elements of air and water from the system.

Now a few words on the metals silver, gold and copper. Learning to wear the correct metal is as important as choosing the appropriate gemstone. Silver is a semi-precious metal that works with the energy of the Moon and it has a negative, yin charge. Silver has the ability to bring what is unconscious into the light of consciousness. Silver is not good for people with excess kapha, but is helpful in treating excessive pitta. Silver does not transmute a negative charge to positive energy, but gold does.

Gold has a positive, yang charge and works with the energy of the Sun. Gold is useful to draw poisons out of the body much as a poultice is used to draw poison out of a boil. This poison, when drawn to the surface, can be transmuted and re-qualified. Gold is more highly evolved than silver and is an effective nerve tonic that improves memory and intelligence. However, gold is counterproductive for individuals with too much pitta, or fire energy.

Copper is poor man's gold. It is used to work with the lower three chakras and bodies and, although not as effective as gold, it too can transmute negative to positive energy, in that it catalyzes and conducts the electrical charge of our thoughts. If we keep our thoughts positive, copper can be a very effective healing agent. It can be helpful in treating the liver, anaemia, spleen and those with excessive kapha.

During my life many gemstones have been my friends and I have been attracted to wear various ones as I needed the qualities they represented. In my twenties I continually wore a green turquoise ring made by the Navaho. This was at a time that I entered my first long-term relationship and, even though I did not know it consciously, I was seeking to open my personal heart, assisted by the turquoise, to this man. In my thirties, as I committed more deeply to spiritual teaching, I sought to eliminate any negativity by wearing a large black tourmaline ring.

In my early forties I was given a cross with four rubies and a sapphire and, as these were given as initiation stones, they had a deeper purpose than healing. In my fifties I felt called to wear large pearls in my ears as they assist me with my female energies and my second chakra, which is perhaps my weakest area. Also, my choice of metal has changed. Whereas in my earlier years I would happily wear silver rings and earrings if I liked the stones they held, now I only wear gold as my essence is more solar than lunar.

Exercise 23: Using Gemstones and Minerals

Take a moment to still your mind before answering the following questions in your journal.

❖ Have you been attracted to different gemstones in the various stages of your life? If so, imagine yourself in these various stages to determine why you needed the qualities of each of these stones.

❖ Which gemstone/metal is healing and strengthening for you at this time? Imagine that you are inside this stone. Become this stone. What qualities do you represent? How does this stone or metal create health or helps you to grow?

❖ Is there a gemstone or metal with which you have no affinity, or even repulsion? What are the reasons for this? Imagine yourself developing a relationship with this stone or metal. What are its gifts?

Crystals and The Crystal Skull

Although many gemstones are crystals, that word is associated normally with the clear quartz crystal—the majority of which are on the blue ray. Crystal is the most highly evolved, growing, breathing life form of the mineral kingdom, and it is capable of clear retention and great clarity in whatever its purpose. Atlanteans used it in their libraries to store information. Crystal can retain information for many thousands of years, which is much longer than a paper book can exist. Also, crystal is friendly to humans who, for eons, have worked with, loved and revered it. The quartz crystal remembers that friendship and desires to serve humanity. This is not the case with many minerals, which are antagonistic to us because of our rape of the mineral kingdom. We have done this through drilling oil, extracting rock from quarries, and mining gems and gold.

It is painful for crystals to be mined by blasting where many of them are killed, or traumatized by this violent method. It is likewise painful for them to be cleaned with corrosive acids and carved into shapes that do not suit their functions.

Just as with the various species of plants, certain varieties of crystals are better able to do some work than others. Herkimer diamonds are good for dream work and midwifing the birth of children. Rose quartz, on the other hand, is tender and sweet like a child, opening the heart to innocent love. Amethysts is helpful to clear away negativity. Single crystals are developing as individuals, while clusters have a group consciousness and are good for holding group energies. Geodes help us to open up and let our beauty shine forth, just as the geode itself looks like a rock from the outside shell and yet holds beautiful crystals within it.

Crystal has been employed since Atlantean times to record information which is still available today. When Atlantis was in danger of turning away from the light, beings from the stars who were overseeing our evolution decided to record information that we would be able to "read" later. They created twelve Crystal Skulls for this purpose. In the early 1900's, Anna Mitchell-Hedges found the most well-known crystal skull on an archaeological dig in British Honduras with her father. That quartz crystal skull, a perfect representation of a human female skull, has been scientifically dated to be at least 12,000 years old.

The Crystal Skulls store knowledge about our Creator, the history of humanity and of the Earth. The skulls were made in Atlantis, although it is more accurate to say that they were seeded on Earth from the stars. Each skull is encoded with information and is almost a living essence of another star as beings from the stars assisted in making the skulls and lent their life essence to them. This is done by downloading the memories from the body elementals of these star beings about their various species into the Crystal Skulls. At this time beings from the stars walked with and taught humans, but they foresaw a time when we would fall below their reach into a lower frequency. They wished to leave us a legacy to point us in their direction. Each skull holds the memory of the entire history of one of these star races, and each skull to some extent knows the history of the twelve stars.

Beings of the inner Earth were also involved in making the Crystal Skulls. Their role was to anchor the energy from the higher dimensions on to the Earth. Working with the co-operation of the crystal's body elemental, they were able to shape the crystal into skulls. The shape of a skull was chosen for several reasons. Skulls are always associated with death, the gateway that separates one level of experience from another. The skulls represent not just physical death, but also the ability to change from one state of consciousness to another and from one set of values to another. If we view death this way, we realize that individuals go through many deaths in one lifetime. To grow spiritually, we undergo not just physical, but also emotional and mental deaths and we must do this consciously.

The second reason that a skull was chosen is that the pineal gland, which is located deep inside the brain where the base of the skull meets the top of the spinal cord in the area called the medulla oblongata, is the gateway to higher dimensions. The pineal gland has crystal life forms in it that grow as we mature. The pineal, not the pituitary as was previously thought by science, is the master gland of the body that is our connection to spirit. Within the pineal gland is contained a *unicell*, which holds the record of the entire history of each individual in relation to the galaxy and the Creator.

Science has assessed that the majority of us currently use a very small part of our brain's capacity. Not a great fact, but the good news is that science is beginning to discover that we can mutate ourselves. I believe this occurs naturally when we access higher frequencies. Then, new information is opened in our pineal gland where it has been stored in the crystal forms waiting for us. The pineal then tells the pituitary what changes it wants in the body. Let's examine instances where this has occurred.

We know that in the majority of humans, only 20 of the 64 codons of our DNA are turned on. According to Drunvalo Melchizedek in his book *The Ancient Secret of the Flower of Life*, several years ago doctors at UCLA studied a boy who had been born with AIDS. He was checked at birth, again at six months and then again at one year of age. He still had AIDS. At age five he was rechecked and the doctors discovered that all traces of AIDS were gone, as if he had never had it. The doctors, as you can imagine, were astounded and in checking how this had happened they discovered that he no longer had the same number of activated codons in his DNA as the majority of humans. He had 24 and his immune system was 3000 times stronger than that of most humans. In fact, he was immune to virtually everything. This boy is not alone. At the time of this study UCLA had found this mutation in 10,000 people.

Not all humans have the same number of chromosomes. Aborigines in Australia and certain tribes in Africa and South America, for example, have 42 + 2 chromosomes whereas the majority of humans presently have 44 +2. Our number of chromosomes, like our cordons, will increase as we enter higher states of consciousness. Presently, science does not know how, and why, these genetic changes occur. The answer to both questions is found in the pineal gland, which increases the number of chromosomes as our frequency increases.

Just as each of us has a unicell, so does Earth. The twelve Crystal Skulls, each one representing one of the twelve rays, are the unicell for Earth. Each skull represents a different function, chakra and frequency for Earth. For example, one skull is clear sight, a second is clear speech, a third is clear feeling, a fourth is clear intent, and a fifth is clear hearing. Anna Mitchell-Hedges' skull represents clear speech. Its purpose is to speak the part of the truth that humanity and other races on Earth need to know at this time. Originally, the skulls were sent with adepts to various places on the planet where they anchored the light of spirit and taught.

I visited Anna Mitchell-Hedges and the Crystal Skull several times. I was invited to touch the Crystal Skull and tell Anna what it had to say. Much of the information in this chapter was given to me by the Crystal Skull. Anna was a perfect guardian for it as she had so much purity in her and yet determination for it to be kept safe.

Visiting the Crystal Skull was synchronistic in many ways for me. It coincided with a growing interest in quartz crystals. They can help increase our love, remove negativity, increase our telepathic gifts and many other things. Wonderful crystals have come to me over the years from many countries of the world and just as easily I have given them to others. We can no more own a crystal than we can own another living being. They have their own consciousness and their special gift is that they work with the etheric body of individuals.

Exercise 24: Getting to Know Your Crystal

Take a moment to still your mind before answering the following questions in your journal.

❖ Choose a crystal that you would like to develop a relationship with for the following exercise. When you first obtain a crystal or gemstone, clean and purify it in a saltwater bath in sunlight, preferably outside, for three days.

❖ Next, while holding the crystal, ask its function.

❖ After completing these steps, use the crystal according to its function and carry your crystal when you wish to do what it is programmed to do. For example, to record information, hold it and think the images into the crystal. To build a stronger image, you might talk the information into it.

❖ This technique requires practice to access the information that we have recorded or that has been recorded. In order to do this, we must be able to attune ourselves to the frequency and essence of the crystal and to build a relationship with it. Crystal gives information through images and sending thoughts.

Section Five

LIFE IN OUR SOLAR SYSTEM

Rainbow Dust

Skirting your issues, circling your core
leads to endless illusion.
But, 'Who am I?' is an arrow
piercing the veil
killing you dead.
Fears of greater and lesser disappear
only 'What is' remains.
Nothing to defend, nor uphold,
only rainbow dust of God everywhere.

Sirius, The Cosmic Dragon and The Pleiades

With billions of stars in our galaxy, it would be sheer arrogance to believe that Earth is the only planet with sentient life. The Earth, which is often called Gaia, is an evolving being as are all the other planets and Sun of our solar system. In fact, our Sun is a relatively young star and there are thousands of solar systems with intelligent life—many of which are in advance of ours. Two of the most important, as far as human evolution is concerned, are Sirius and the Pleiades.

Sirius is at a higher level of evolution than our Sun and, like the Pleiades, it is involved in humanity's evolution. The ancient Egyptians, the Dogon of Africa, and many other cultures recognized its importance, and the Egyptians called Sirius the "Great Provider". Both the Egyptians and Dogons, in addition to their lunar calendar for agricultural purposes, had a second calendar, based on the 365.25 days in a Sirian year, which was used for civil and religious events. The Sirian calendar was as sophisticated as that of our present day. The calculations were made on July 23rd each year when, after a couple of months of being out of sight, Sirius arose almost due east for only one minute before our Sun's rising. This alignment was so important in ancient Egypt that it was used in almost all of their temples and even the gaze of the Sphinx followed this alignment.

Modern astronomy reveals that Sirius is a binary or double star with one vast low density half (Sirius A) and one smaller, extremely dense half (Sirius B). According to Robert Temple in his book *The Sirian Mystery*, the Dogon of Africa speak of a third star (Sirius C) in the Sirian system. Astronomers only confirmed this third star in 1995 although the Dogon knew of it for at least 700 years prior to that. The Dogon, who could not possibly have seen this third star with the naked eye, called it, *Emme ya*, which means the "Sun of Women".

The Dogon believed that the starting point of creation was Sirius B, which revolves around Sirius A. They called Sirius B the Digitaria star and said that it was the smallest and heaviest of all stars and contained the germ of all things. Western science believes that Sirius B is a white dwarf and recent estimates indicate that one cubic inch of white dwarfs weigh approximately 1.5 million tons. Excluding black holes, this makes white dwarfs the heaviest matter in the universe. The Dogons also believed that Sirius's movement on its own axis upheld all creation in space. A white dwarf—because of its massive gravitational pull—would have this effect on its neighbours.

Dogons knew that it took close to fifty years for Sirius B to rotate around Sirius A—a fact only discovered in the last twenty years by western astronomers. In fact, astronomers did not even discover Sirius B until 1862, although Dogon cave paintings over 700 years old detail this information. Dogons also knew about the outer planets of our solar system, Neptune, Pluto and Uranus, which the western world has discovered only more recently. Even more interesting is the fact that the Dogons knew what the planets looked liked when approached from space.

So how is it that the Dogons, ancient Egyptians, and others knew information about Sirius that we have rediscovered only much later in the western world? Could it be because these cultures remembered contact with Sirians at an earlier time in human evolution?

Ancient Egyptians called Sirius *the eye of Ra*, (Ra being the name they gave to the Creator) and, although they knew that Sirius was not Ra, they believed that Sirius was related to the Creator. Furthermore, ancient Egyptians spoke of both Sirius A, which they linked to their chief goddess Isis and Sirius B, which they linked to their head god Osiris. Sirius C, following this thought, would be the equivalent of Horus, the child of Isis and Osiris. The ancient Egyptians believed that Isis, Osiris and Horus brought civilization and learning to the Earth. As mentioned earlier, these three beings, along with others, came to Earth, at least as early as Atlantean times, to teach humans the principles that would develop into consciousness.

In earlier times twelve visible planets orbited Sirius. They have since become the dense white dwarf star that circles Sirius. This absorption of planets happens to solar systems as they evolve in consciousness, and our Sun will ultimately absorb the planets in our solar system as well. Even after the absorption occurs, the consciousness of the twelve planets remains in higher realms.

Twelve beings—the heads of each of the twelve planets that used to revolve around the Sirian Sun—form a governing council on Sirius. The twelve represent humanity's brothers and sisters and they interact with our evolution. The head of the council is Lord Sirius who, like a Phoenix, is a composite of masculine, feminine, and neutral qualities and who has the ability to die and re-birth himself. His body, composed of all colours of the rainbow, illustrates how he has become, through his own transmutation, the embodiment of all twelve rays of creation. Lord Sirius works under the auspices of the same one that we know as our Creator, who is the consciousness of our galaxy. Lord Sirius feeds the beings, which he has been involved with creating and nurturing, even as the mythical Phoenix takes the blood from its own breast to feed its children. Humanity is one of these children of Lord Sirius.

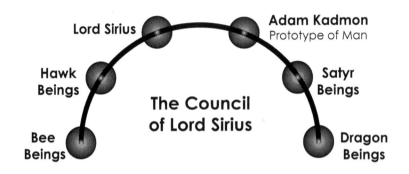

Figure 13 - Although there are twelve in the Council of Lord Sirius, only five are mentioned here.

Twelve prototypes of different races sit on the Sirian council, and Adam Kadmon, the prototype of Humanity, is one of these. Adam Kadmon is the counterpart of Eve who evolved in the Pleiades, although she, like Adam, is still a daughter of Sirius. Many of these beings are found in human myths.

For example, a Hawk-like being that North American aboriginals call Eagle and the ancient Egyptians refer to as Horus is on the council. These species of advanced beings are not the same as the species of birds on our planet known as hawks and eagles. This Hawk-like group started its evolution at a similar time as the Els and has come from a different organ of the Creator than the Els. Its gifts are far and clear sight and it can see the future and the past and is able to exist simultaneously in the present, past, and future. Because of its clear sight these Hawk beings assist other species to discover their own truth by reflecting back to them—almost as a mirror does—who they are. Dr. Jim Hurtak, in *The Keys of Enoch*, writes that the Hawk beings come from the star Arcturus. They create evolved life forms in our galaxy by way of genetic manipulation and in accordance with the divine plan.

The Hawk beings prefer to be alone. However, some entered human evolution, with permission from those who oversee our evolution, as hawk-human hybrids to experience being part of a group, being dependent, and joining with others. Human hybrids from this Hawk group might feel discomfort in the human body and might seek hybrids from other evolutions to share its experience. During this joining, this Hawk being sees the history of our planet, and of its entire species, and it saves this memory to share with other sentient groups.

Another life form on the council resembles a Bee. Its skin is alive and exudes scents and luminescence. It is able to pick up feelings from others and to be both a receiver and sender of communication. There are hybrid humans of this Bee species also. They are often highly sensitive to the frequencies of others and love the senses of touch and taste while, at the same time, they might be overwhelmed when others touch them.

A fourth being on the Sirian council looks like our image of Satan. He has cloven hooves like a goat standing on two legs, two horns, a tail and red eyes. This group of beings works a great deal with the emotional body and the fire element. They are no more inherently evil than are humans. In dreams and in altered states of consciousness, individuals have seen the image of this being telepathically, and thought erroneously that they had seen the devil. In Greek myths this being is Pan, the goat-like randy god who lusts after nymphs, although in his higher form he is the god of music and wine. In the South-Western United States the native people refer to him as Kokopelli who, like Pan, plays the flute and uses the kundalini energy for creativity, sexuality, pleasure and spiritual transformation. Pan is helping the elementals on the Earth with their evolution. There are Satyr-human hybrids evolving on the Earth who have the characteristics described here.

Another species of beings represented on the Sirian council is the Dragon and it, like the Hawk-like beings, has impacted human evolution. Dragons are a species of great wisdom and long life who come from a different solar system than ours and who are often called upon to judge other races. They are cold-blooded and have not acquired love to the same extent as most evolved species. Some Dragons have come to Earth to develop this quality because, without love, there might be misjudgments and miscalculations in their wisdom. With compassion, Dragons will be able to vivify their decisions—to make them living and not static laws. The Creator's laws, after all, evolve and change from one age to another as the species which these laws serve evolve.

Earth myths recall the great wisdom of Dragons and how it is difficult for humans to surpass them in logical discussion. Dragons came to Earth in previous evolutions when Earth's atmosphere was not as heavy as now. They, like the Hawk-like beings, no longer live in Earth's third dimension, but still exist in higher dimensions.

There are several ways in which Dragons help humanity. Dragons are known to breathe fire and the Creator's Word is living fire. The Dragon speaks with the fire of purest truth, which allows it to be a judge for other beings like humanity. The Dragon, also known as the snake, is associated with the snake in the Garden of Eden who tempted Eve to eat of the tree of knowledge. Knowledge is a lower form of wisdom. The Dragon ultimately shows humanity the path to this wisdom.

The Dragon is also associated with the kundalini energy, represented in Hindu and Oriental traditions as a snake. This sexual, creative, healing and spiritual energy moves through our chakras up a central channel located along our spine to produce enlightenment. The Earth also has kundalini energy, which moves along its electromagnetic leylines, also known as dragon lines, and this energy enables Earth to rise in consciousness.

Dragons have entered human evolution and the hybrids have many qualities described here. These include wisdom, the ability to discern the truth, sexuality, a gift in healing and spirituality. They might also been drawn to the arcane arts and need to guard against pride and feelings of superiority.

A great Cosmic Dragon, who is very highly evolved, is presently affecting our solar system, as its function is to assist Earth in its birth into the collective body of conscious planets. The symbol of this process is found in the Chinese tradition as the Dragon that encircles the Cosmic Egg. Currently, the Cosmic Dragon is brooding Gaia. The shell of the Egg, which is the ring-pass-not that surrounds the Earth, is starting to crack. This Cosmic Dragon has the responsibility to open the ring-pass-not, which protects beings on other planets in our solar system and beings from other stars from humans, and us from them. This opening will occur when Gaia is welcomed as a conscious planet.

The Cosmic Dragon is bringing new cosmic energies into our solar system. They might appear chaotic, as they are foreign to our existing status quo. The Cosmic Dragon gathers the substances from the etheric that are needed in the new age that we are entering. It activates our higher chakras so that we are able to enter this new state in our evolution. It works with the Karmic Board to judge exactly when the unicell in our pineal gland needs to be opened to awaken our dormant DNA. In this way, humanity will be readied to access the cosmic information that has not been available to it until now.

The above-mentioned beings live and work within manifested worlds and sit on the left side of Sirius. Like our own Sun, Sirius has undergone many cycles in its evolution, and only the beings with whom humans have been and will be interacting are mentioned here. Lord Sirius placed these beings on planets in various solar systems and many so-called "humans" are originally from these evolutions. It is beyond the scope of this book to speak of the other beings on the Sirian council who exist in higher dimensions and in the Void.

The Pleiades, like Earth, is a child of the Sirian solar system and in many ways it is in advance of us. In the Pleiadian system there are twelve stars; seven clearly visible to the naked eye and five less visible. The Pleiades have worked with Earth in the realms of colour, music, smell, and touch, to activate sensual experiences for our learning and pleasure. This gift has served both as a temptation to humans and also as an awakener of the emotional body, which will ultimately develop our faculty for love.

References to Pleiadians are found in the myths of many civilisations on Earth. Many Mediterranean cultures believe that knowledge was brought from the stars by dolphin-like beings who breathed air, lived in the water, and had fish-like tails. These creation stories also are found amongst the Dogon of Africa and the Uros

Indians who live on Lake Titicaca in Bolivia. Pleiadians have helped to create dolphin evolution on Earth, and dolphins are the yin part of the human race—that which brings grace, compassion, gentleness and beauty. There are also dolphin-human hybrids, as mentioned previously in the section on Lemuria.

I'd like to share a story with you about how the Cosmic Dragon is influencing us presently. A few years ago our institute organized a summer camp for children and their families, and it was especially helpful for children who had spiritual experiences. In one visualization exercise I asked both adults and children to discover an elemental who wished to work with them. The adults shared their experiences first and they had received all manner of fairies, brownies and elves to work with. When the children shared their experiences, each one of them had received a dragon. What was especially unusual about this was that neither I nor any other person had made reference to dragons during the week.

The children's dragons came in all shapes and sizes and each was able to speak with the children telepathically and tell them what qualities they had and how they were helping each child. In the circle was an autistic teenager by the name of Michael who had not spoken with any of us during the week.

I asked, "Michael, did you receive a dragon?"

He nodded, "Yes".

"Would you like to tell us about it?" I asked.

Again he nodded "Yes" and turned to his mother and whispered his story for her to share with the group.

Michael's dragon was large and blue and protected him and as he shared I had a strong sense that it was connected to Archangel Michael. In fact, in all the children's stories it was clear that they were being contacted by aspects of the Great Cosmic Dragon which needs helpers during these coming years of the birth of the New Earth. By the way, since Michael received his dragon he has overcome much of his autism and is functioning much better in the world.

**Exercise 25: Your Connection
with Sirius, The Pleiades and The Cosmic Dragon**

*Take a moment to still your mind before answering the following
questions in your journal.*

❖ Can you identify with Sirius or the Pleiades? If so, how do
you experience the gifts from these stars?

❖ Do you recognize these gifts in other individuals? In whom
and in what way?

❖ Have you had an experience with the Cosmic Dragon? If
so, what is its purpose in your life?

The Sun

Astronomers acknowledge that our solar system is part of the more
evolved solar system of Sirius and that the Sirian system, in turn,
revolves around the Great Central Sun of our galaxy. According to
Hindu cosmology it takes 225 million years for our solar system to make
a complete clockwise circuit around the Great Central Sun, which is
referred to as one year in the life of Brahman. Unseen spiritual light
streams from the super massive black hole that is this Great Central
Sun lying at the heart of the galaxy. When we learn more about the
galaxy we will likely discover that there are twelve evolving systems
revolving around the Central Sun.

The principle of twelve to one was discussed in the first section of
this book. It has been mentioned that there are twelve chakras, twelve
dimensions, twelve rays of energy and that each teacher, such as Jesus,
has twelve students for whom he/she is responsible. It is necessary to
elaborate on this principle as it exists at the very centre of all life and
is the way in which solar systems are constructed.

Even human reproduction is dependent on this principle as it has
recently been discovered that twelve sperm are necessary to fertilize
the egg. It appears that ten, eleven or twelve sperm form a pattern on
the surface of the egg, which allows the twelfth sperm to enter. The

egg is yin and has a positive polarity, while the sperm is yang and has a negative polarity. These two polarities must be equal for fertilization to occur. The egg seems to know exactly what she needs in order to balance the negative and positive polarities and science has proven that the egg chooses the sperm that will enter to fertilize her.

This same principle of twelve to one exists in our solar system, with the Sun as the egg and the planets as the sperm. The Sun is a balance of all polarities as its Greek name Helios and Vesta connotes. Some of the twelve planets carry a more yang (masculine) charge, and others a more yin (feminine) charge. This same principle exists with sperm, some will produce females and others males. All evolving life forms learn to balance the duality of the yin and yang, positive and negative polarities of the twelve chakras, rays, and dimensions. When they do this, they can produce life by themselves. This is what our Sun has learned to do.

Suns have great intelligence, but it is an intelligence unlike ours. Fire elementals, called Salamanders, over a lengthy evolution evolve into the physical body of the Sun. The Salamander's purpose is to create fire on all planes of existence, including in our human bodies. This evolution is very difficult and involves several deviations from pure elemental evolution in order to acquire the necessary qualities. In the early states of development a Sun learns to hold a pattern for long ages of time. Next, a budding Sun must learn to work consciously to hold its physical, emotional, mental and higher spiritual bodies together. This takes eons and Suns are very old. After Suns have finished that state of their evolution, some elect to become black holes, portals that allow travel between solar systems and galaxies.

It may be difficult to believe that the Sun, Earth and all planets are beings of great intelligence, far surpassing that of a human. In our third dimensional existence we are acculturated to believe that things lacking human faces lack intelligence. This belief, which has led us to exploit other life forms, is now changing and many of us now know our Earth by her original Greek name Gaia. Naming Gaia has personalized her. Once we are able to embrace the concept of a living, conscious Earth, it is only a small step to embrace the Sun as an even more evolved form of consciousness. From this point, it's inevitable that sooner or later we will realise that these celestial bodies are parts of our Creator. The Earth is a part of the body of the Sun of our solar system, as the Sun is a part of the body of Sirius that, in turn, is part of the body of the Great Central Sun.

The Sun that we see with our eyes is only the physical body of the greater being that is know esoterically as Helios and Vesta. Our Sun receives energy from the Great Central Sun, our Creator, who is referred to esoterically by its Greek name Alpha and Omega, meaning the beginning and end. This energy is food for both our Sun and all life on its planets. In Hindu scripture this energy is referred to as prana. Prana, which is intelligent and finer than atomic energy, is cosmic vibration sustaining all life.

The Sun distributes prana by way of Salamanders who bring this energy to Earth. Each being is given what is healthy for it and, as we evolve, we are given more energy from the Sun to distribute to others as food. This energy moves through all of our chakras and most especially through the pineal gland. We also receive energy from the Earth through our root and feet chakras, which then travels up through our bodies. Ideally, these energies move through our body with no restriction and exit through all chakras, especially through the heart, which beams unconditional love to all beings. Individuals whose frequency is on the fifth level of consciousness no longer require any food other than prana in order to live.

Just as each of us is composed of the Earth, so each of us is composed of the Sun. Christianity speaks about God the Father, God the Son, and God the Holy Spirit. This Trinity is found in the threefold flame in each of our hearts representing divine will, love–wisdom, and active intelligence. Each of us left the Creator with a small flame in our hearts. This flame grows as we evolve spiritually from being a spark initially to being all flame as we awaken. This flame is our inner Sun.

Although diet is an important component of maintaining physical health as we increase our frequency, in many ways the activities we engage in are more important. During spiritual transformation most individuals need quiet, calm and rest and to be in an environment of positive individuals. Many things might happen for which there is no outer explanation and we need time to adjust to these changes.

One such situation happened to me when I was about thirty. I underwent a very strange time where I would drift out of this third dimensional reality and into the Void. I would sit on the sofa for hours beside the phone attempting to remember who I was wanting to call. Then I'd drive the car to do errands and would not be able to remember how to get home. When I spoke to my closest friends and common-law partner Bill about this it was difficult for them to believe me as I looked normal and was able to speak articulately and also they knew me as a well-functioning person in the world.

One day Bill and I were lined up to see a new film. I was in the line for folks who had their tickets and he was in line to purchase the tickets. My line started to move and before I knew it I was inside the theatre having passed the ticket checkers by mistake. I went and got a seat and waited. Bill did not appear. Finally I left the theatre to find him and, when I did, explained that I was invisible and the ticket checker had not seen me. Bill laughed as if he didn't quite believe me and said, "I bet you can't do that again." I replied, "I'll see you inside." I walked past the same ticket checkers again and they did not see me. Just as the film started Bill appeared and said, that his line had been closed at the person before him and the only reason he got in was that I was inside with two seats. I think he started to believe something was happening to me after this event.

Exercise 26: Your Physical Transformation

Take a moment to still your mind before answering the following questions in your journal.

❖ Have you noticed a change in the foods you consume from childhood to the present? If so, what are the changes?

❖ Have you noticed a change in the ways you receive energy from your physical environment, other people, situations? What energizes and de-energizes you?

❖ Are there other physical, emotional, mental, or spiritual changes, which you have noted, that indicate an increase in your frequency?

Life on Planets in our Solar System

We discover a great deal about the history of our solar system through ancient Sumerian and Babylonian records. Sumerian texts, which are our oldest written records going back 5800 years, revealed that the Earth tilted on its axis 23 degrees, orbited the Sun, and that it took 25,920 years to do a grand circle (the time it takes for Earth to do a full circle so that the Earth's North Pole points at the same North Star).

Tibetans and Hindus call these particular cycles *yugas*. Each yuga has both an ascending and descending phase. In an ascending phase, we awaken, learn and expand and during a descending phase we are asleep, let go of what we learned in the previous cycle, and contract. In the microcosm of our own life, we enter an ascending phase at birth, continue to learn and grow until late middle age when we enter a descending phase, release what we no longer need, become forgetful, and then die. The cycle continues with our rebirth into a new life, while we forget about the previous life. Presently, Earth is leaving a *Kali Yuga*, or descending phase, and is at the beginning of an ascending, awakening phase. History shows no recollection of this ancient information because we lose the memory of previous cycles during our descending phase.

I believe that there are twelve planetary bodies in our solar system. Each one specializes in a specific quality and all twelve qualities are necessary for our Sun to be a Creator. Astronomers currently acknowledge nine planets to which I add the moon, asteroid belt and one other.

Mercury

Mercury is the closest "acknowledged" planet to the Sun and, along with Pluto, it is one of the smallest planets. The Greeks and Romans thought of the god Mercury either as a divine child or as an androgynous young man. The inhabitants of Mercury have an androgynous nature, and as a chemical substance mercury is very good for balancing the male and female polarities. Mercury takes his directions from the Sun, who in the Greek pantheon is Zeus. The Greeks depicted Mercury with wings on his feet and, as befits his role, he communicates the Sun's will throughout the solar system and acts as a mediator and counsellor to the other planets. This is also the role of the fifth chakra.

Our Solar System

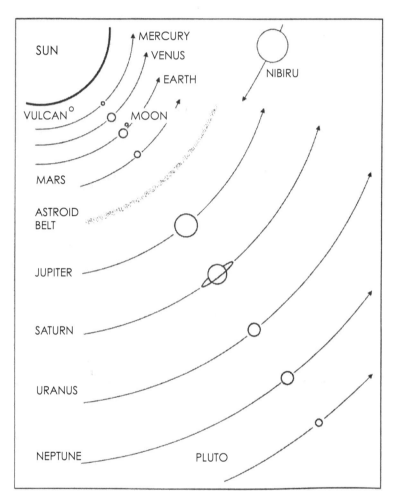

Figure 14 - Twelve planetary bodies in our solar system

Mars

Mars has yang energy and represents the first chakra, which is the physical will to live. Science tells us that Mars once had oceans, lakes and rivers much like Earth. Its landmass, in fact, is about the same size as that of Earth. Scientists maintain that there are no life forms on Mars but this conclusion is due to only looking in the third dimension for intelligent life inhabiting Mars. Martian physical existence is at a lower frequency than that of Earth. Actually, Martians exist in a second dimension. Furthermore, our second and their second dimension are not identical.

The frequency of Mars is a half-tone lower than Earth's. The Martian emotional dimension overlaps Earth's physical dimension. The emotional body of Mars has long affected Earth with the negative qualities of belligerence, aggressiveness, bestiality, and lust. Martins also have a kind of pigheadedness that does not allow for a new thought or a new way of doing something. The average Martian is unable to help the average human evolve, for most are behind our evolution. Their positive qualities are not in as great abundance, for Martian development of the positive is not as strong as their working through of the negative. Yet fierce loyalty, supreme trust, and unwavering dedication to a goal are some of the positive Martian qualities. They have great courage and self-sacrifice when they believe in something.

Inhabitants of some planets in our solar system, especially Venusians and Martians, have incarnated on Earth to learn various qualities. Attracted to military professions, Martians are natural soldiers. They might also gravitate towards police or rescue work, such as ambulance driving and fire fighting, where their action-oriented personalities find positive expression. They work better in environments where there are specific rules to follow. With a good leader who gives them positive laws to follow, they will evolve quite quickly. They do not do well dealing with abstract questions such as, "What is my purpose in life?" As children, some Martians have problems in school because they are given too much freedom. They excel in structured environments.

Venus

Venus originally represented the second chakra for our solar system. Venus is the planet of relationships and love, and originally she was concerned with personal love. At the present time, Venus, who has a yin charge, exemplifies the quality of non-possessive, detached love. Venus, as the heart of this solar system, works with the 3000 plus asteroids that lie between Mars and Jupiter. Among these are four large asteroids, Ceres, the asteroid belt's only dwarf planet, is about 950 kilometers in diameter. These asteroids were originally intended to become a larger planet but as a result of a collision early in the development of our solar system they have become as they are now. They still hold the orbital place separating the inner planets in our solar system from the outer planets.

Both Earth and the Moon were gravely damaged in the cataclysm that caused the asteroids. It was when this happened that the planet Venus decided to look after the Earth. Its Lord, Sanat Kumara, came to Earth until humanity was able to control its own evolution. This has now transpired, but the Moon is still being assisted by Sanat Kumara of Venus to evolve the quality of love. All planets represent a different chakra for our solar system. Venus is currently working with the heart chakra, but Venusians are presently evolving their mind to work with the fifth chakra, at the throat. Venus' love is the spiritual soul love for all living beings.

Venusians are concerned with service for others and when they incarnate as hybrids on Earth they bring this quality. They are attracted to professions that will better the Earth. These could be humanistic areas such as social work, counselling and teaching, or spiritual areas, ecology, astronomy and medicine. For Venusians, it is not so much the profession that is important, but the motivation of service that lies behind their choice.

If Venusians and Martians incarnate in human evolution, they only bring a part of their original evolution into their Earth incarnation. They do this with the permission of the Karmic Board of their planet and each planet has a council of twelve that decides on the evolution of their planet. There is also a council of twelve that oversees the collective evolution of all planets in our solar system. Each planet has a representative on this council; Buddha represents Earth, Sanat Kumara represents Venus, Poseidon represents Neptune.

Humans also incarnate on other planets to learn qualities, or to share what Earth's strengths are. This is not common before humans become Ascended Masters, but quite common after that time. This exchange of planetary inhabitants doesn't necessarily occur in the third dimension, but often happens in higher planes of existence. Inhabitants of Jupiter, for example, teach some of Earth's Ascended Masters, and the two groups are in continual communication on higher frequencies.

The Moon

The Moon, like the asteroid belt, was meant to develop as an independent planet. During the same catastrophe when the asteroid belt was created the primitive Earth and the Moon were damaged. This happened when a large body about the size of Mars entered our solar system from space and collided with our primitive Earth, cleaving it in two. One piece became the Earth and the second piece became the Moon, which is one-quarter the size of the Earth.

Scientific evidence substantiates this. NASA has discovered from rock samples that the Moon was once a living planet. Like Earth, the Moon is layered, which means that it solidified from its own original molten state where it generated its own heat. There is also evidence that the ancient rocks of the Moon were magnetized and that the magnetic fields were changed or reversed. Its mineral composition, very similar to that of Earth, indicates an early relationship. Scientists have discovered that the Moon evolved normally for hundreds of millions of years, then 4.5 billion years ago a cataclysmic event happened when celestial bodies crashed into it.

The Moon is very much alive but its evolution has changed since the collision. The Moon's focus is a lower form of love, the love of our personality. This is why people associate being in love with the Moon. The Moon has taken over Venus's function of holding personal love in the second chakra, leaving Venus to hold the heart energy of the fourth chakra.

During the Lemurian cycle, Earth was not able to continue her evolution as the Laggards built up a great deal of negativity. The ones who were overseeing human evolution even questioned if we would be allowed to continue our evolution on this planet. The Moon offered, with Sanat Kumara's assistance, to hold much of this negativity so that humans and the Earth could continue their evolution. It was arranged that during the full Moon a part of our negative karma would be given back to the Earth for humans to transmute. This is why, during the full Moon, people become so emotionally unstable and why more crimes of violence and passion occur than at any other time.

The Moon's name is Luna. The word lunatic refers to a person who is emotionally unstable and crazed by the Moon. This is a current characteristic of the Moon. Luna has not yet stabilized her emotional and mental bodies so she is unable to support life on her physical body.

When we entered the Aquarian Age, the Moon increased the amount of negativity that she was giving back to Earth. As she releases this negativity, she stabilizes her own emotional and mental bodies. Luna is finishing her apprenticeship with Venus and is once again becoming self-sufficient. She must now strengthen her bodies to enter the new age that awaits Earth. The Sun gives the Moon energy to transport negativity to Earth and without this support, the Moon could not do this. The Sun also lends energy to all conscious beings working on Earth who help with the transmutation process.

The Earth will become a fully conscious planet when she has absorbed all of her karma. In the third dimension we will witness more wars, global conflict, family violence and environmental difficulties as she does this over these next two thousand years. Just as each of us individually must pay off our karma, so must the Moon and the Earth. The Moon made a great sacrifice by holding the karma of Earth and humanity for so long. By doing so the Moon has accelerated her evolution and development of love. Even so, the Moon is in a primitive state of evolution in comparison with the other planets.

Jupiter

The inhabitants of Jupiter, the largest planet in the solar system, work consciously with the law of expansion and contraction, work that is essential for budding suns. With its four moons, Jupiter is a budding sun and therefore everything that has been described in the chapter on the Sun will apply to Jupiter in time. Jupiter is more yang, and represents the sixth chakra and the quality of intuition for our solar system.

Saturn

Saturn represents the seventh chakra and the ability to move in space and time. The space between the rings and body of Saturn is very significant. This space is a gateway to the Void, an area of no space and no time, and the inhabitants of Saturn are able to visit other planets by using the different frequencies of the rings. The rings around the body of Saturn are like electrons spinning around a proton. An electron continually spins around a proton attracted by the magnetism of the proton; you see that same principle demonstrated by Saturn. Inhabitants of Saturn work with the function of stillness and movement. If we were to cultivate an inner stillness, we would have that same magnetic attraction in our nature as Saturn does. We would attract everything to us that we need and space and time would be at our command.

Planets and Their Qualities

Planet	Quality
Vulcan	Kundalini fire
Mercury	Communication
Venus	Divine love, relationship
Moon	Personal love
Earth	Free will
Mars	Passions, loyalty, courage
Asteroid Belt	Scattered thoughts
Nibiru	Technological/scientific aptitude
Jupiter	Principle of expansion
Saturn	Principle of movement, time & space
Uranus	Higher mental
Neptune	Higher love
Pluto	Atomic magnetism

Figure 15 - Summary chart of planetary qualities.

Uranus

The outer planets, birthed later, represent the higher spiritual chakras. Jupiter and Saturn birthed Uranus through magnetism, gravity and centrifugal force in the depths of cosmological time, however Uranus was not discovered by western astronomers until 1781. Uranus represents the eight chakra and spiritual consciousness of our solar system. Humanity is unable to understand this consciousness at present.

Neptune

Similarly astronomers did not discover Neptune until 1846. Neptune is governed by Lord Poseidon who has often come to Earth to assist with dolphin, whale and fish evolution. Some inhabitants evolving on Neptune are like mermen and mermaids. Although they are not human, their characteristics are more like those of humans than fish. They are a conscious, water-breathing race evolving in an astral world that is different from the astral frequency of Earth. Neptune's waters are heavier than the air, but lighter than the water of Earth. It is like a cloud of rain that is condensing and this has a most refreshing effect on the inhabitants of Neptune, whose greatest test is to balance the air and water elements.

Pluto

Pluto, the most recent planet discovered by western astronomers, is small and heavy. Pluto holds the balance between the Void and the positive reality for this solar system. To work with Plutonian energy, one must learn to balance its constructive and destructive elements, as the inhabitants of Pluto do. As beings, they are half-dark negatively charged and half-light positively charged so their very bodies are vehicles for their work and function. Plutonium is employed to create nuclear fission in the physical world and humans must also create the equivalent of a nuclear reaction in order to access the other realities where the inhabitants of Pluto have their being. At the beginning of the 21st century astronomers are contesting the legitimacy of Pluto as a planet.

The Twelfth Planet: Nibiru or Vulcan?

And what of a twelfth planet? Zacharia Sitchin, author of *The 12th Planet*, would have us believe that there is a planet, Nibiru, about the size of Jupiter that moves retrograde to all the other planet's orbits and only enters our system every 3600 years, coming in by way of Neptune. Although his theory has a large following among lay people, experts in related disciplines dispute the accuracy of Sitchin's information. If what he says is true then we could encounter this retrograde planet again in several hundred years.

Hindu astrology also makes reference to two invisible planets. The first planet is called Rahu, or the Dragon's head, and is translated in Western astrology as the node of the Moon. The second planet Ketu, or the Dragon's tail, is exactly 180 degrees distant from the Dragon's head. According to Hindu astrology both of these invisible planets move in a retrograde motion and are very powerful. Could this Dragon be the same planet Sitchin refers to? Could it be the Cosmic Dragon that was discussed earlier that is overseeing the birth of the Earth at this time? Are these possibilities both true or could the twelfth planet be something else?

A third hypothesis was postulated in 1859 by French mathematician Urbain Le Verrier who claimed there was a small planet inside the orbit of Mercury that was closest to the Sun. He called this planet Vulcan after the Roman god of beneficial and nonbeneficial fire. Given that Le Verrier used the same techniques in discovering Vulcan that he employed in discovering Neptune, he does deserve a hearing. Many astronomers until Le Verrier's death in 1877 claimed to have seen a red planet moving against the Sun. However, because of the extreme difficulty of seeing it against the bright background of the Sun and its small size, no definite proof has been found. Still, even to our present day there are people who claim to have seen Vulcan, in the location Le Urbain suggests.

The qualities associated with Vulcan are the transmutation of baser metals to the higher and of the personality into the beauty of the soul. This is the function of the kundalini fire energy.

It is recommended that the critical reader examine the information on these unacknowledged planets for him or herself or we can wait for the universe to let us know the truth in its own timing. Ultimately, all twelve planets will be absorbed into the Sun, just as in human evolution the lower bodies of our personality will be absorbed into the higher bodies of our soul.

The question, "Is there a twelfth planet and, if so, where is it?" has been the most difficult for me to discuss and I have not released this book for many years waiting for "the truth" to unveil itself. Spiritual information involves an ethical responsibility for accuracy. However, that being said, I feel it is essential to give individuals the information in this book, as it is needed now. So I ask you to help me journey with this question. What I do know is that there is a twelfth planet. I feel, sense, this strongly. What I do not know for certain is if this planet exists in a physical dimension in our solar system, for the physical dimension is not necessary in order to carry an energy that influences us.

Exercise 27: You and Other Planets

Take a moment to still your mind before answering the following questions in your journal.

❖ Do you feel drawn to any planet other than Earth? If so, what is your relationship with this planet?

❖ Do you know any individuals who might be hybrids from other planets? If so, who are they and how can you assist them in their evolution on Earth?

Birth of the New Earth

Major changes are affecting the entire solar system and not just the Earth. Astronomers tell us that the cores of spiral galaxies, like our Milky Way, periodically emit cosmic and gamma waves equal to millions of supernova explosions (the explosions caused by individual suns in the last phase of their life.) These cosmic rays travel at close to the speed of light. One of these galactic emissions could strike our solar system without warning and be seen only as a bright blue light coming from the Galactic Center in the constellation Sagittarius. According to astrophysicist Paul La Violette in his book *Earth under Fire*, this last happened 12,000 to 13,000 years ago. One of these emissions would increase solar flares a thousandfold, burn our forests, ignite volcanoes and cause a new Ice Age.

Sam Solanki of the Max Plank Institute in Germany has stated that the Sun is more violently active now than at any time in the past 11,000 years and that solar flares are increasing. Dr. Dimitriev and the Russian National Academy of Science report that the heliosphere, which is the magnetic "egg" around the Sun, is affecting our entire solar system, having increased tenfold over the last 15 or 20 years. They indicate that it is currently overheating, and also the Sun is heating up.

When the first human landed on the Moon in 1969 they reported no atmosphere. Since then a new atmosphere is growing which is now 6,000 kilometers deep. NASA discovered in 1997 through its Mars Observer probe that the Martian atmosphere was twice that which they had thought. Venus, Jupiter, Uranus and Neptune are also noticeably brighter than they used to be. The magnetic field of Jupiter has more than doubled and Neptune's is likewise increasing.

We know that, like the Sun, the Earth is also heating up. We call it global warming. The rate at which glaciers are now melting has never occurred in Earth's known history. Our temperatures are on a massive incline. Moving to a colder or warmer part of the Earth will not save us from this devastation, as the entire Earth is affected. The Earth is physically overheating and her mechanism for regulating her temperature is breaking down. Oceanographers call it the "great conveyor belt" and they have discovered that it is responsible for keeping the tropics cool and temperate climates warm. This conveyor belt is powered by the naturally higher amount of salt in the northern seas. As the icecaps melt due to global warming the salinity decreases which slows the conveyor belt. Lately this belt has stopped and restarted a few times. Should it break down completely it would conceivably not move for between a few hundred to a few thousand years, initiating a new Ice Age.

In addition, the Earth is overheating due to volcanic activity. The Russian National Academy of Science reports that overall volcanic activity has increased 500 percent within the past hundred years and is increasing exponentially. Volcanoes are classified on a scale measuring from 1 to 8 on the Volcanic Explosivity Index with VEI 8 volcanoes referred to as super volcanoes. Super volcanoes, both underwater and on land, are capable of creating a volcanic winter, even ending civilizations as seen by the eruption of the super volcano of VEI 6 on Santorini around 1500 BCE. It spewed ash as far away as Egypt, Crete and Turkey that probably caused the decline of those civilizations through the resulting plague and famine.

One of the largest volcanoes in the world is in Yellowstone National Park and it still erupts every 600,000 to 700,000 years. The last major eruption was 640,000 years ago. According to Lawrence Joseph in his book, *Apocalypse 2012*, the caldera has risen three-quarters of a meter since 1922 and is filling with magma, an indication that it is getting ready to explode again. Yellowstone, a VEI 8, feeds off vast reserves of uranium underneath the Earth 's surface. Geologist Robert Smith of the University of Utah states that its explosion would be the equivalent of 1000 Hiroshima type atom bombs per second. This would plunge the entire Western hemisphere into a volcanic nuclear winter from which we would never recover.

Meanwhile, the Earth's magnetic field is steeply decreasing, which in the past has signalled a pole shift. The magnetic field runs not only through the Earth but creates lines of force surrounding the Earth. This field acts as a protective shield for repelling excessive solar and cosmic radiation. Unfortunately, this field is at its lowest point in 2000 years. If the magnetic field reaches zero point the poles of the Earth reverse. Polar reversals occur regularly every 12,000 years with the most recent reversal occurring 12,000 years ago. Between Patagonia and the Cape of Good Hope lies the "South Atlantic anomaly" where the magnetic field already moves in the opposite direction. It is possible that when the magnetism of the Earth reverses that the spin could reverse as well. If this happened it would likely tear apart landmasses, creating gigantic tidal waves and volcanism, destroying civilization as we know it.

At first glance, this scientific data appears negative, because life as we know it will end. The positive side is that our entire solar system is moving to a higher state of consciousness. The Galactic Center, the Great Central Sun, is alive and has a heartbeat with a cycle of every 12,000 years. We humans are linked to the Galactic Center, the one we think of as our Creator, and we are in unity with it in multidimensional levels including that of the physical. The events transpiring on the Sun and Earth currently are not in isolation and are not the initial cause but a response to a call from the Great Central Sun for us to evolve into the next stage of consciousness.

The Earth, called in Greek Gaia, and humans are linked in an evolutionary spiral that leads to becoming increasingly conscious. Both

Gaia and her human inhabitants have reached a place in their evolution where a quantum jump is taking place. The next two thousand years, which is known as the Aquarian Age, is the time of the enlightened human, the water bearer who pours the water of life on the Earth.

We have come to the point in history when we can move from linear to multidimensional time. This is how it works. Our bodies are electromagnetic entities aligned to the magnetic fields of the Earth. Our memories, through our etheric body template, are also held in place with the memory systems of the Earth, what we call the Akashic records, morphogenetic fields, noosphere or collective unconscious. A magnetic pole reversal will have the effect of erasing all previous programming for the Earth and also for us individually. This occurred in previous ages and this is why there is no record of previous high civilizations such as Atlantis.

The Earth is made up mostly of silica compounds. Silica is the material used to store information in computer chips. When a computer crash occurs the memory is erased from our hard drive. We might be able to recover a fragment, which is why we remember a bit about Atlantis, but we lose the program in its totality. We know that solar storms and high voltage flashes such as lightning or atomic blasts blow up the fine crystal structures in silica chips, so we can imagine what an immense burst of solar and galactic energy would do to our entire communication grid of TV's, radios, cell phones and computers. A solar storm also blasts off our atmosphere just as a puff of air will remove the dust from a book. There is one theory that this might be what happened to Mars at an earlier time.

Just as energy on the Sun has an immense impact on our physical reality, it has this same effect on erasing the memories for our collective unconscious in the etheric field of the Earth.

We know scientifically that the frequency of the Earth, the "Schumann resonance" is increasing, which is assisting us to move to higher octaves, higher dimensions. This has been a gradually increasing process. But when the former magnetic field collapses we will instantaneously find ourselves in whatever frequency we are resonating with at that time. This is why Buddhists speak about the importance of dying consciously, for when people die they find themselves in the dimension of the frequency of their thoughts. When the poles reverse we have choices about which dimension we can go to. This allows for masses of humans, if they are open to seeing these new possibilities, to be in the fourth, fifth or even sixth dimensions. If, however, they cannot hold that energy and are still attracted to lower thoughts and feelings they will drift down again into lower frequencies in the very unpleasant third dimension remaining after the pole reversal. This is not unlike what happens when we die. There are many heavens available to us. Some will play golf, others will continue spiritual work and study. We go to where our thoughts direct us. Those who choose to relinquish the limitations of the little self to merge with the Divine will have a light body, the physical-etheric body where they can move consciously in time and space between dimensions. Our home world at that time will be only one choice available with other planets and dimensions also open to individuals.

As may be remembered, Stephen Hawking believes that there are two laws that govern the universe. The law of evolution controlling space and time, and the no-boundary condition, which exists outside of time without beginning or end. In the Christian tradition this sounds like the difference between karma and the law of grace. Karma is that we reap what we sow, even if it takes many lifetimes to see this. Grace is the law of love that as soon as we repent of our negative beliefs or actions we can rise to a higher dimension. Both these laws will affect the Earth and us during this time of change.

In the third dimension, which is controlled by time, we see a massive cleansing going on. Yet, in an instant, if our thoughts are in higher frequencies we have the opportunity to rise to higher dimensions during this time of transition. In the fourth dimension we must learn to control our negative emotions and release feelings such as lust, greed, anger, impatience, jealousy, scarcity, fear, depression, self-importance. Then we rise to the fifth dimension where we will be telepathically in communion with all other beings. We must learn to control our thoughts lest we pollute the fifth dimension with wandering thoughts. Focus, concentration, purity of motivation and compassion will all be very important. In the next two thousand or so years humanity will be learning to control the mental and emotional realms to be co-creators and guardians on this planet.

It's imperative that we realize that every cell of our body is part of the Earth. Approximately 70 percent of Gaia's surface is covered with water and the amount of water in a mature human is also 70 percent. This could be a coincidence, however that is unlikely. Distanced from our Mother Earth, as we are, we also forget another fundamental truth, which is that every bit of our food is alive too. Every part of our bodies is constructed out of the building blocks absorbed from the bodies of other life forms. Every cubic centimeter of soil and sediment teems with billions of microorganisms. Gaia's life and ours are one. If we forget this, we forget our purpose.

Humans are meant to create with the Earth a beautiful world in alignment with divine law. To do this we must move to higher dimensions and frequencies. These are accessed through the positive emotions of joy, trust, faith, gratitude and compassion. Conversely, negative feelings of anger, frustration, fear and greed lower our frequency.

Presently, the Moon carries all the negative karma that was created on the planet through various cycles of evolution. The Earth would not be able to evolve with the weight of this karma, and so the Moon offered to carry it. To evolve to the fourth and fifth levels of consciousness both the Earth and individual humans must transmute all their negative karma.

So that we are not overwhelmed with negativity, the Karmic Board allows only a piece of this negativity to reincarnate with each individual. Likewise, the Governing Board for this solar system allows only a piece of the negative karma, which the Moon is carrying for us, to be worked on in each cycle of two thousand years. Now that we have entered the Age of St. Germain, the age of transmutation by the violet fire, much more of both our individual and planetary negativity can be transmuted.

Before the Earth can enter its next state of evolution, it needs to undergo a massive cleansing. This physical cleansing may take many forms, such as shifting land plates that will lead to increased volcanic activity, floods and temperature rises. Various kinds of fire will burn up the Earth's last remaining karma. During this cleansing many beings may die, just as plants and trees are killed during a forest fire. However, this cleansing also re-fertilizes the soil for the next cycle of growth. This is true for forests and also for our planet and her inhabitants.

There are also emotional and mental cleansings taking place on Earth, which result in economic and communication collapses and war. Each time a crisis happens it is harder to resolve because there is so much pressure and backlog that has built up to bring about a major cleansing of Earth. The backlog of negativity that we have created through war, pollution, and negative thoughtforms acts against our fellow humans and other Earth species.

It is preferable for the Earth to cleanse herself gradually rather than through a major healing crisis like a war. We humans are given every opportunity to cleanse ourselves before the Earth moves into her new frequency, so that as many individuals as possible are able to make the transition. Our physical, etheric, emotional and mental bodies must be cleansed and lightened from the weight of negativity that exists in the third and fourth dimensions before we can live in the fifth dimension. Thousands every day come to the point of transition but slip back. The more positive our thoughts and feelings, the less chance that we'll need to undergo a major physical cleansing. It is not that we completely escape the cleansing process, but that its severity is minimized so, for example, we get a bad cold instead of cancer.

Most evolving species undergo a severe healing crisis in their evolution. It is the major test by fire that occurs both in the macrocosm of a planet and in the life of an individual. Therefore, individuals go through a time in their evolution when they encounter their personal nuclear war. In fact, sometimes our incessant fear of nuclear war occurs because we are encountering our own inner war in the process of cleansing and renewal. We must welcome these opportunities for growth, as there is no longer time for resting on our laurels thinking, "I've done it."

As the Earth increases her frequency, people may become increasingly unstable emotionally. We might find ourselves becoming more frustrated or angry as the cleansing fire of the Cosmic Dragon burns our dross. So what can we do? We can ground ourselves by walking on the earth. We can work with the fire of transmutation given to us by St. Germain to dissolve unwanted negative patterns. As we do this, our ability to hold more fire increases and the three-fold flame of love, wisdom and divine will burns brighter in our hearts. When in doubt, love others more, serve more, forgive ourselves more, and be more patient with ourselves.

To prepare for the Earth's birth as a conscious planet we must awaken as well. The best way to ensure our evolution on Earth is to purify ourselves physically, emotionally, and mentally, and to develop our heart as a vehicle to serve others. It is not too late. There are many who are borderline and who, with extra effort, would be able to bring themselves up to the point where they may continue their evolution on the new Earth.

If we do not cleanse our mental and emotional toxicity, a healing crisis will arise in the physical. This is our body saying, "I won't take any more garbage." When we become ill, the body starts cleansing itself. To assist it, we need to add only the ingredients that will best help the body to detoxify, stabilize and be nourished. The best healers are sunlight, breathing fresh air, moderate exercise, eating green plants and drinking a lot of good water to clean out the body. And, of course, keeping our thoughts positive towards others and ourselves.

Sometimes, a strange thing happens. When we begin to correct our negative thoughts and feelings or when we start exercising or fasting, we become ill. Most often, what is happening is that the body has cleansed itself in the present and is now cleansing its past build-up of garbage. Still, it is best to always consult one's inner self about how to heal oneself. We can greatly increase our effectiveness by asking the Angels, the Ascended Masters and the Creator to assist us with this process. By praying with power and faith, we attract them to us. All of us were meant to enjoy perfect health. We can live much longer lives and our physical body need not decay as it does now. In future, we will be able to live in harmony with the Earth and divine law, and be able to leave our bodies with ease when it is time to move from one state to another. Advanced yogis can do this even now.

Currently we use only 3 to 5 percent of our DNA and the rest is called "Junk DNA". Is it possible that this DNA merely needs to be called into action by higher mental functions that we have not yet evolved? As our frequency changes, transforming us from a caterpillar into a butterfly, there are many physical symptoms that may arise. These could include dizziness, heat problems with kundalini openings, skin irritations, migraines, joint pains, immune system breakdowns, extreme fatigue or anxiety, fevers and heart palpitations. Sometimes there are bliss experiences and sometimes intense physical or psychological agony, or both. These symptoms are transitory and will change.

This is the body transforming from a caterpillar into a butterfly, and the one needs die for the other to be born. Clinging to the old body or way of life will not work. This is the dark night of the soul, or as I prefer to say, the dark night of the personality, and it may last for weeks, months, years or even a lifetime. It lasts as long as is needed for the transition to be made.

Seeing the pollution, murder and greed on our suffering Earth, the situation might appear hopeless. But none of us is ever given more than we can handle. Some people buckle under the stress and others rise to the challenge and work consciously, in many ways, to assist others with their transmutation. This process is quickening now, and more of our negative karma is being absorbed from the fourth dimension. It will take approximately two thousand years before the Earth is able to fully enter the fifth dimension at which time all Earth inhabitants will be able to live at the higher frequency. There are many individuals and species that will not be able to do this. So what will happen with them?

Many species of animals and some humans and plants, but not in their Earth form, will be taken to other planets and solar systems to continue their evolution. This is not an unusual process. Many of Earth's plants and humans are hybrids that originated in other solar systems. Some humans who have not overcome their bellicose qualities will go to Mars where they will again have opportunities to overcome anger. Other individuals, who have been on the Earth for many cycles and who still drown themselves in the emotions, will be taken to Neptune, a water planet, to work on this particular element.

It is not expected that humans who have incarnated for just a few thousand years should be able to achieve control of their emotions and their astral body. But humans who have been on Earth for hundreds of thousands of years and are still unable to overcome their emotions hold back the cycle of evolution. These individuals are taken off the Earth, with their etheric body and blueprint adjusted so they are able to exist on other planets and solar systems. They will not lose the essence of their humanity or the memory of all they have been on Earth. They will be hybrids. Let's hope that these Laggards will reform and not contaminate their new homes, as many did who came to Earth.

After people have transmuted their personal karma, they commence working on the collective karma of all humanity. There are many light workers on the planet who are doing just this, which happens when we are able to stabilize our own emotional mental bodies in the third and fourth stage of transformation.

Although humanity as a whole has not done this, Gaia has. When Gaia purified her heart and emptied herself of I, me, mine, she evolved to a place where she could ignite with the flame from her own heart the threefold flame of light, love and divine will that resides in the heart of each being. She is now able to feed all the bodies—including the spiritual ones—of the beings evolving on her. Gaia is ready to move from the equivalent of her solar plexus to her heart chakra in her evolution.

To assist our Mother Earth through her birth, we can clean her waters and air and take care of all her animals, plants and all forms of life. Each of us needs to take responsibility for doing this in our own lives. Many of us will be called to professions that focus on assisting the physical body of the Earth. We each have the responsibility to leave her in better health than when we were born. Our successes and failures are recorded in our Book of Life and our karma is affected by how responsibly we do this.

Some individuals assist in the physical element, in recycling, organic farming and peace initiatives. Others work in the emotional element, in counselling and psychotherapy to help individuals get past their fears to discover the real purpose of their lives. Others work with the mental body by helping the mentally ill and those people who wish to break through their emotional body into their mental body, so they can become conscious co-creators. Each of these groups assists others to strengthen their good qualities and to take responsibility for their thoughts and actions. Even though this current trial is very difficult and painful, it is encouraging to see how many individuals are making this effort.

Nor are we alone with this process. There are many beings from outside our solar system that affect humanity and there are still others that we think of as UFOs. The vast majority of UFO sightings are not clouds or weather abnormalities. They are crafts inhabited by intelligent races who have come and are coming from other solar systems, and a few from other galaxies, to witness the birth of the Earth and to welcome her into sisterhood and adulthood with them.

These are not enemies. Quite the contrary, they are beings who have developed into adulthood with their own gifts and are welcoming our efforts to do the same. They will not interfere with the Earth, as she must do this herself. Extraterrestrials remind us of what we will become and encourage us to raise our frequency to join them. Some, although not all, could come to Earth without spacecraft, but not in their physical bodies, as their physical bodies are too refined and too many frequencies above the Earth for them to live in physical bodies here. Many have come before as visitors and even as active supporters for humanity. Some have even taken humans to other planets and solar systems in our dream state.

Other extraterrestrials have come as scientists, or inquirers to witness the process unfolding on Earth. Not all kinds of extraterrestrials are at the same level of evolution. Some are only slightly more evolved than humanity, although their technologies are superior to ours and allow interstellar travel. Just as human scientists explore genetic manipulation and do tests on primitive animals, some of these extraterrestrial scientists have done tests on humans. Some alien scientists have come to reap their harvest from other cycles. Some, even in this cycle, have seeded the Earth with different species for one purpose or another. Some have been ambassadors for altruistic purposes to assist humanity; others have been sent as punishment so they might learn a lesson. Not all of these species are advanced spiritually. Although they are able to travel in space and time, it does not necessarily follow that they have developed their spiritual gifts to the same degree as their technical prowess.

Some extraterrestrials have created the crop circles in Britain and Canada. They are able to create complex patterns in a field of grain in just a few minutes by reversing polarities and altering gravity. Many people report that they feel nauseous inside crop circles because it affects their equilibrium, as the energy polarities are not usual for them. In these fields of wheat or barley, the wheat is not cut but bent in different directions to weave these complex patterns. The crop circle patterns have increased in complexity from when they first started.

The patterns are mathematical symbols meant to teach us higher mathematical principles.

Spacecraft can enter the third and fourth planes of existence, and even the Void. But most often interstellar spacecraft travel occurs in the fifth, sixth and seventh planes as extraterrestrials do not wish to be seen by humans. Yet, on a super-conscious level, most people know of their existence. The instruments in these spacecrafts allow the travellers to tell what is happening on both lower and higher planes of existence. In many cases the spaceships are stationed at the intersection points of a grid that surrounds the Earth. Existing in all dimensions, this grid is like a spider web. It is basically an etheric crystalline structure with an electromagnetic component that spacecraft use.

Power points are created on the grid where energies from different poles intersect. Spacecraft remain at these intersection points on the grid to conserve energy and to use the natural flow of energy for communication. Also, they are able to move quickly from one intersection point on the grid to another. Interstellar craft use the grid system around the planet to move between dimensions. To travel to other solar systems, they use the black hole through our Sun, which is the negative polarity of the Sun. The smaller landing craft use just the grid system, but the larger space vehicles need to use the black holes.

Some spacecraft that fly in lower dimensions are relatively small. They are scout craft. Others are medium in size. There are very large ones, which transport the smaller craft from one solar system to another, from one galaxy to another. Some of the mid-size craft could move on their own from solar system to solar system, but it takes more energy. Also, they lack both comfort and the research facilities to process the information that they have acquired. Some UFOs go into the inner Earth where there are landing stations. The inhabitants of the inner Earth are traffic controllers who monitor extraterrestrial traffic. They know which interstellar species are on Earth at present and what their purpose is. They document it all. They are the customs people who gather reports and record this information through crystals.

Many people have seen UFOs and my mother is among them. My mother lived in the country far from city lights and one day when I was visiting she mentioned her sightings—plural—to me. My first reaction, I am embarrassed to say, was that her eyes were going however I decided to postpone judgment. Some hours later, glancing out the window, she called to me, "Come quick, it's back." Opening the back door we saw a bright, spherical object in the night sky. This object hovered but there was no sound as it moved silently and slowly up and down in the sky. Suddenly, it moved so quickly that is was gone in a second.

Individuals who have had a similar experience know that this object is a UFO and no amount of contrary statements from scientists and governments stating that it is a helicopter or a weather balloon will convince them. Perhaps you also have seen a UFO or had an experience with an extraterrestrial. If so, has this changed your views of reality? For me it is proof that humans are a young species in our destiny as traveller's to the stars.

A few extraterrestrials have entered Earth evolution with permission from the Karmic Board of humanity. The humans who host these extraterrestrials have agreed to do so before birth, knowing that this will quicken and develop qualities that are latent or underdeveloped in humans. For most, this is considered an honour. This process is not technically difficult. Earth's scientists are working with similar things even now. It is like taking blood, a cell, or a piece of genetic material and implanting it in the body, emotions and mind of the human host who is incarnating. What is difficult is knowing the correct timing, amount and individual to implant and doing this within the pattern of evolution. Also, there is always a danger that the extraterrestrial will lose its own consciousness. Therefore, human hosts must be of such a development that it is possible for the extraterrestrials to maintain consciousness when they are in that body.

Another method evolved beings may employ to incarnate on the Earth is to take over a body in good working order, from a human who no longer wants it. These are the walk-ins that have been mentioned by writers such as Ruth Montgomery. Advanced humans as well as other beings can be walk-ins. In fact, it is easier for humans to inhabit a human body than for beings of other evolutions. Much emotional and mental training of the walk-in is done prior to the actual physical joining. Only the strong, dedicated or those who have much to gain do this because an individual of one species must overcome its natural resistance to inhabiting the bodies of another species.

Human hybrids, who have forgotten their original evolution, are beginning to remember and are searching for both their purpose and their real evolution. Even if we are fully human, we must still learn tolerance and understanding of other species in the Creator's plan. It's essential to remember that there is no better and no worse in evolution. All of us must discover the truth of our existence and maintain a calm acceptance of who we are. We must know our strengths and weaknesses to better help animals, plants and minerals, as well as the other species who have come to Earth. This is the collective purpose of humans.

As I am writing my final words for *Decoding Your Destiny* environmental, social, economic and organizational breakdowns have increased dramatically. My friends, family and co-workers are encountering massive stress as they struggle to make sense of their lives as they are fired, are abandoned by their spouse of twenty-five years, and become seriously ill. On one level these experiences do not make sense but to the Divine they make perfect sense in our transformation.

You also may be going through many difficulties such as these, and I send you love and peaceful thoughts. The important thing to remember is that we are not doing anything wrong or have to change anything in ourselves if these events transpire. This is a time of chaos, the Void between the old order and the new one that is emerging. Be kind to yourself and others. Do not cling to what wants to go and celebrate the Earth, your life and all beings. This is what I am doing and I hope you will join me on this incredible journey that we are on. How lucky we are to be alive in a physical body at this time.

Exercise 28: Your Relationship with the Earth

Take a moment to still your mind before answering the following questions in your journal.

❖ What signs have you noticed that the Earth is going through a massive change?

❖ How have these changes affected you?

❖ How have you been cooperating with the Earth on this process? In your personal life, your work, volunteerism etc.

❖ Are there other ways for you to co-create with the Earth?

Afterword

What a wonderful time to be alive when humanity, our planet and our solar system are awakening from a long sleep of unconsciousness. It is my hope that with the exercises and information offered in this book you will be able to discover your own destiny and see how it relates to humanity and the Earth. We must continue to hope that humanity will meet the challenge of the present and that the dire predictions and agonies of the Earth are the impetus to catalyze our ongoing evolution. We are at a crossroads and the choices we make on a daily basis allow us to change EVERYTHING. Every thought, every feeling, every action counts. We are incredible creators and we can co-create our future with the both Spirit and the Earth here and now. This is our birthright.

We can do it.

Appendix
Twelve Rays of Creation

What are rays? We are familiar with the idea of our sun emitting rays of light. These rays are reflected as the spectrum of colour in our manifested world, or as the colours of a rainbow. The seven visible colours are each on a different ray of energy.

Our galaxy is actually made up of twelve rays of energy, and the other five rays are unseen by our human eye as they are on higher frequencies. Each ray has a certain quality, and different life forms have strengths on one of these rays.

To become full co-creators we must learn to work with all twelve rays of energy. Once we have learned to do this, at least with a working knowledge, our focus becomes the three main rays, which work through the heart. These are divine will, love-wisdom and active intelligence. As we progress further along the spiritual path these three rays dissolve into one—the first ray of divine will. Divine will means total uncompromising commitment to world service and to manifesting the Creator's plan on Earth. All co-creators ultimately must work with this ray.

Many esoteric writers have written books on the rays. Some, such as Alice Bailey as channelled from Djwhal Khul, *The Rays and the Initiations* and a compilation by one of her students *The Seven Rays of Life*, are very detailed accounts of these rays.

Each ray has a specific frequency, a certain note, much like the white and black keys on a piano. Colours, resembling the colours of the rainbow, are associated with these notes. Life is created by sound, which is frequency. We can no more take away one frequency than remove one colour from the rainbow or one organ from our body. For physical, emotional, mental and spiritual health we need all twelve frequencies.

The first ray that flows from our Creator is divine will that starts all creation from an idea. The second ray is the dual energy of love-wisdom and we can think of it as the wisdom of compassion. Some Great Ones such as Buddha embody primarily the wisdom aspect and some such as Christ the love aspect of the second ray. The second ray is the ray of the master builder who takes the Creator's idea and creates a plan to actualize it. The third ray is active intelligence and adaptability. This ray is concerned with the tools, building forces that must be employed to actualize the plan of the first and second rays. To do this the third ray subdivides itself into five minor rays, which are ray four—harmony, beauty, and art; ray five—science and concrete knowledge; ray six—devotion and idealism; ray seven—transformation, ceremonial order and magic.

Twelve Rays of Creation

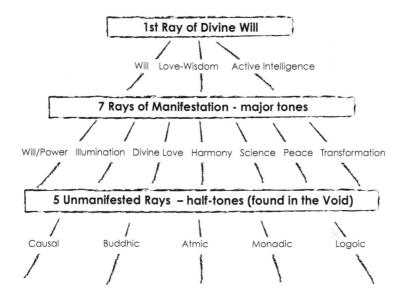

Figure 16 - Rays of Creation and their attributes

There are colours identified with these rays however attributing colours can be confusing as they interweave continually and vary depending from which dimension they are viewed. For example, the first ray of will can be seen as red from the physical dimension although in higher realms it is blue. Just as a fire turns from red to blue as its heat increases, so the first ray of will in the physical dimension is seen mostly as the red of passion and power, but in higher realms the first ray is the cool blue of detached will.

Not much is written about the five unmanifested rays that are found in the Void although some spiritual teachers, such as Alice

Bailey and Dyhani Yahoo have made mention to these energies in various ways. One hundred years ago Rudolph Steiner, a mystic and the founder of anthroposophy, said that only seven Masters—one on each of the seven rays—incarnate at a time, and that the other five remain in the Void unseen and, by most, unknown. In the same way, we see only the seven primary colours of light and not the five that exist in the Void in higher realms.

The five invisible rays are accessed through higher consciousness. The first unmanifested, the eighth ray, is on the higher mental plane of the causal, soul body. This ray is accessible through an opening of the third eye chakra, which commonly occurs after the third state in spiritual transformation. This is referred to as the dark night of the soul when we decide to continue on our spiritual journey even if it is painful. This is characterized by feeling alone, cut off from the Divine and also others, and dissatisfaction with the material world. This is what Jesus undergoes in the garden of Gethsemane.

The second unmanifested, or ninth ray is the Buddhic, which we encounter through sacrifice and opening of the heart chakra during the fourth state of spiritual transformation. This is exemplified during the Jesus crucifixion when he forgave those who crucified him, while at the same time giving of himself totally to help others.

The third unmanifested, or tenth ray is the Atmic. We encounter this energy during the fifth state of transformation when our kundalini energy moves from the bottom of the spine up through the crown chakra and we are awakened. This involves a complete surrender to let our ego, the personality, that is the separate self, die. Jesus illustrates this when he ascended three days after the death of his physical body.

The fourth unmanifested, or eleventh ray is the Monadic, which according to Alice Bailey is accessible after the sixth state of consciousness and is related to the throat chakra. I agree with Rudolph Steiner who states that this eleventh ray works with the Holy Spirit.

The fifth unmanifested, or twelfth ray, is the Logoic. Bailey says this is related to the crown chakra and that it is open after the seventh state of spiritual transformation. Steiner relates this twelfth ray to the Christ, the Son of the Great Central Sun and this is congruent with my perception.

Primary Sources

Grant, *Hellinistic Religions*, Bobbs-Merrill, Indianapolis, 1953.

Graham Hancock, *Underworld, The Mysterious Origins of Civilization*, Three Rivers Press, New York, 2003.

Kings James version of *The Bible, Collins, New York, 1953.*

W. G. Lambert and A. R. Millard, *Atra-Hasis: the Babylonian Story of the Flood*

B. Layton, *The Gnostic Scriptures*, SCM Press Ltd., London, 1987.

N. K. Sanders, *Poems of Heaven and Hell from Ancient Mesopotamia*, Penguin, New York, 1971.

Scientific American, Special Edition, *New Look at Human Evolution*, August 2003.

Recommended Reading

Larry Arnold, *Ablaze: The mysterious fires of spontaneous human combustion*, M. Evans Company, New York, 1995.

Alice Bailey, *Cosmic Fire*, Lucis Publishing Co., New York, 1973.

Alice Bailey, *Initiation, Human and Solar*, Lucis Publishing Co., New York, 1973.

Alice Bailey, *Esoteric Psychology Vol. 1 and 11*, Lucis Publishing Co., New York, 1970.

Alice Bailey, *The Rays and the Initiations*, Lucis Publishing Co., New York, 1976.

Alice Bailey, *The Seven Rays of Life*, compiled by a student of Alice Bailey and Djwhal Khul, Lucis Publishing Co., New York, 1995.

William Bloom,, *Devas, Fairies and Angels: A Modern Approach*, Gothic Image Publications, Glastonbury, 1986.

Gregg Braden, *Walking Between the Worlds, and Awakening to Zero Point*, Videos and Book, Conscious Wave Inc., Broomfield Colorado, 1998.

Sophie Burnham, *A Book of Angels*, Galantine Books, New York, 1990.

Masuru Emoto, *The Messages of Water*, Hado Kyoikusha, 1999.

Masuru Emoto, *The Hidden Messages in Water*, Beyond Word Pub., Hillsboro, 2002.

Temple Grandin, *Animals in Translation*, Schreibner, New York, 2006.

Tanis Helliwell, *Take Your Soul to Work*, Random House, Toronto, 1999.

Tanis Helliwell, *Summer with the Leprechauns: The authorized edition*, Wayshower Enterprises, Vancouver, 1997, 2011.

Tanis Helliwell, *Pilgrimage with by the Leprechauns: A True Story of a Mystical Tour of Ireland*, Wayshower Enterprises, Vancouver, 2009.

Tanis Helliwell, *Embraced by Love*, Wayshower Enterprises, Vancouver, 2008, 2012.

Geoffrey Hodgson, *Kingdom of the Gods*, Theosophical Publishing House, Wheaton.

Geoffrey Hodgson, *A Brotherhood of Angels and Men,* Quest Books, Wheaton, 1927.

J. J. Hurtak, *The Book of Knowledge: The Keys of Enoch,* 1982.

Anodea Judith, *Wheels of Life,* Llewellyn Publications, St. Paul, 1997.

Leonard William King, *The Seven Tablets of Creation,* London, 1902.

Samuel Noah Kramer, *Sumerian Mythology,* Greenwood Press, 1988.

C.W. Leadbeater, *Chakras,* Theosophical Publishing House, Wheaton, 1979.

C.W. Leadbeater, *Invisible Helpers,* Theosophical Publishing House, Wheaton, 1896.

C.W. Leadbeater, *Thoughtforms and Astral Plane,* Theosophical Publishing House, Wheaton, 1979.

John Uri Lloyd, *Etidorhpa,* Pocket Books, New York, 1978.

Drunvalo Melchizedek, *The Ancient Secret of the Flower of Life,* Light Technology Publishing, Flagstaff, 1990.

Franklin Merrell-Wolff, *Pathways Through to Space,* Julian Press, New York, 1973.

Jeffrey Moussaieff, *When Elephants Weep,* Delta Book, New York, 1996.

Patanjali, *How to Know God: The Yoga Aphorisms of Patanjali,* translated by Swami Prabhavananda and Christopher Isherwood, Vedanta Press, CA, 1953.

Helena Roerich, *Agni Yoga, Hierarchy, Heart, The Fiery World,* Agni Yoga Society, New York.

N.K. Sanders, *Poems of Heaven and Hell from Ancient Mesopotamia,* Penguin, London, 1971.

R. A. Schwaller de Lubicz , *The Temple Within Man,* Autumn Books, USA, 1977.

Shankara, *Crest Jewel of Discrimination,* translated by Swami Prabhavananda and Christopher Isherwood, Vedanta Press, CA, 1978.

Rupert Sheldrake, *Dogs that know when their owners are coming home,* Three Rivers Press, New York, 2011.

Zecharia Sitchin, *The 12th Planet,* Avon Books, New York, 1978.

Sri Aurobindo, *A Greater Psychology,* Jeremy P. Tarcher/Putnam, New York, 2001.

Rudolf Steiner, *Cosmic Memory,* Rudolf Steiner Publications, Blauvelt, New York, 1976.

Rudolf Steiner, *How to Know Higher Worlds,* Anthroposophic Press, Great Barrington, MA, 1994.

Rudolf Steiner, *The Influence of Spiritual Beings upon Man,* Anthroposophical Press, Hudson, 1982.

Rudolf Steiner, *The Spiritual Hierarchies,* Anthroposophical Press, Hudson, 1983.

Rudolf Steiner, *Theosophy,* Anthroposophical Press, Great Barrington, 1994.

David Suzuki, *The Sacred Balance, Rediscovering our Place in Nature,* Greystone Books, Vancouver, 1997.

Robert Temple, *The Sirius Mystery,* Destiny Books, Rochester, 1998.

Two Disciples, *Rainbow Bridge 11*, New Age Press, Berkeley, 1981.

Paramahansa Yogananda, *The Autobiography of a Yogi*, Self-Realization Fellowship, Los Angeles,1946.

Paramahansa Yogananda, *The Divine Romance*, Self-Realization Fellowship, Los Angeles, 1986

Paramahansa Yogananda, *Man's Eternal Quest*, Self-Realization Fellowship, Los Angeles, 1982.

Paramahansa Yogananda, *Journey into Self-Realization*, Self-Realization Fellowship, Los Angeles,1997.

Paramahansa Yogananda, *God Talks with Arjuna: The Bhagavad Gita*, Self-Realization Fellowship, Los Angeles,1995.

John Anthony West, *Serpent in the Sky*, Theosophical Publishing House, Wheaton, 1993.

Ken Wilbur, *A Brief History of Everything*, Shambhala, Boston, 1996.

Ken Wilbur, *Transformation of Consciousness*, cowritten with Jack Engler & Daniel Brown, Shambhala, Boston, 1986.

About the Author

Tanis Helliwell, M.Ed. is the founder of the International Institute for Transformation (IIT), which since January 2000 has offered programs to assist individuals to become conscious creators to work with the spiritual laws that govern our world. Tanis, a mystic in the modern world, has brought spiritual consciousness into the mainstream for over 30 years.

Tanis is the author of *Summer with the Leprechauns, Pilgrimage with the Leprechauns, Embraced by Love* and *Take Your Soul to Work*. Her DVDs, *Elementals and Nature Spirits* and *Spiritual Transformation: Journey of Co-creation*, as well as her 9 CDs on the *Inner Mysteries* are helpful to individuals who want to work with elementals and other sentient beings evolving on Earth.

She is a student and teacher of the Inner Mysteries, living on the seacoast north of Vancouver, Canada. Since childhood, she has seen and heard elementals, angels, and master teachers in higher dimensions. For 16 years she conducted a therapy practice, helping individuals with their spiritual transformation. As well, to heal the Earth and to catalyze individual transformation she has led tours and walking pilgrimages to sacred sites for over twenty years.

Tanis Helliwell is a sought after keynote speaker whose insightful awareness is applied in a variety of spiritual disciplines. She has presented at conferences also featuring Rupert Sheldrake, Matthew Fox, Barbara Marx Hubbard, Gregg Braden, Fritjof Capra, and Jean Houston. These conferences include The Science and Consciousness Conference in Albuquerque, The World Future Society in Washington, DC; and Spirit and Business conferences in Boston, Toronto, Vancouver and Mexico. Tanis has also presented at Findhorn, Hollyhock, A.R.E. Edgar Cayce and Alice Bailey conferences.

In addition to her therapy practice and spiritual workshops and tours, she worked for almost thirty years as a consultant to business, universities, and government, to catalyze organizational transformation and to help individuals develop their potential. Her work is committed to helping people to develop right relationships with themselves, others and the Earth.

To write to the author, order books, CDs and DVDs, or for information on upcoming workshops, please contact:

Tanis Helliwell
1766 Hollingsworth Rd.,
Powell River, BC., Canada V8A 0M4
E-mail: tanis@tanishelliwell.com
Web sites: www.tanishelliwell.com/ www.iitransform.com
www.facebook.com/Tanis.Helliwell

BOOKS:
Summer with the Leprechauns: the authorized edition
Pilgrimage with the Leprechauns: a true story of a mystical tour of Ireland
Decoding Your Destiny: keys to humanity's spiritual transformation
Take Your Soul to Work
Embraced by Love

DVDs:
1. Elementals and Nature Spirits
2. Spiritual Transformation: Journey of Co-creation
3. Take Your Soul to Work
4. Managing the Stress of Change

CDs
Series A - Personal Growth Collection: 2 visualizations
1. Path of Your Life / Your Favourite Place
2. Eliminating Negativity / Purpose of Your Life
3. Linking Up World Servers / Healing the Earth

Series B - Mysteries Collection: Talk and visualization
1. Reawakening Ancestral Memory / Between the Worlds
2. The Celtic Mysteries / Quest for the Holy Grail
3. The Egyptian Mysteries / Initiation in the Pyramid of Giza
4. The Greek Mysteries / Your Male and Female Archetypes
5. The Christian Mysteries / Jesus Life: A Story of Initiation
6. Address from The Earth/ Manifesting Peace on Earth

Made in the USA
Lexington, KY
03 April 2015